Alan R. Capon

Triumphant JOURNEY

The TCS Story

The TCS Group
Trenton, Ontario

*"It is not the beginning of a great enterprise
but rather the seeing of it through to a full conclusion
that bringeth the true honour."*

– Sir Francis Drake

Triumphant Journey
The TCS Story
Copyright © 2006 Alan R. Capon
ISBN 0-919825-55-9

Printed by Printcraft, Picton, Ontario.

CONTENTS

This book is dedicated to
Jeanie Fraser James
wife of Eben James I,
and
Gwen Mayne James
wife of Eben James II,
who, behind the scenes, each
made a major contribution
to the success of TCS.

FOREWORD

I am honoured to write this Foreword because of the high regard I have for the late Eben James.

I grew up with the James family on Henry Street and went to school with the eldest daughter, Joan, who was a very attractive and brilliant student who entered McGill University in her 15th year.

The last child in the close-knit family was Mawnan F. James who was not expected to live. Those were the days before antibiotics and modern medicine but the legendary Nurse Shannick moved in with the family for four months. The baby lived and was always referred to as "Babe".

His two other children were Eben, who took over management of the company when his father died, and Margot, a bright, intelligent girl.

In the summers in the 1920's, our families rented primitive cottages on Papineau Lake, which was a daylong drive from Trenton over rough dirt roads and winding hills.

Mr. James drove a large Hudson car with vigour and the cottage people would ask what day he was coming north. Meeting Mr. James at the top of one of those hills could be a problem as it was said Mr. James liked his half of the road in the middle.

The long drive north proved onerous for the parents who eventually bought cottage land on Lake Ontario and have been there ever since.

The cottages were situated on a bank overlooking a sand beach on Lake Ontario. Mr. James had a daily swim. He would leave his cottage, walk across the beach to the water, discard his bathing suit and slowly wade out in Lake Ontario "au naturel". It was not long before the matrons in the other cottages would ask "did you see Mr. James this morning?"

With most issues for Mr. James it was mostly black and white. He suggested to his family that they do the right thing and ignore public opinion.

He was devoted to his church where he donated a barrel of holly every Christmas, and had a strong and ongoing interest in the old country.

As later years approached and he was in ill health, he was heard to remark on occasion "that he hadn't had a good game of bridge in 10 years and he had buried all his friends". On another occasion, he commented, "this business of keeping old people alive is the biggest farce in the world today".

For years, he was president of the local branch of the Conservative Party and a great supporter. This created an unusual situation. His wife, Jeanie Fraser, who he loved dearly, was a staunch Liberal and sister of the late Senator Bill Fraser. The story is with validity, that one parent would baby-sit while the other went out to vote in the other direction.

He was deeply involved in the procuring and exporting of apples and made in excess of 55 trips to the United Kingdom.

Eben James Sr., was a very colourful figure and we are unlikely to see his equal again.

- WAYNE SIMMONS

INTRODUCTION

Few companies reach their 100th year and even fewer achieve this milestone under the guidance of the third generation of the founding family.

Trenton Cold Storage, or the TCS Group, as it is known today, was founded in 1902 by the first Eben James as The Apple and Produce Cold Storage and Forwarding Company Limited. Its purpose was to pack, store and ship barrels of apples from Ontario to the United Kingdom.

Through the years, the company faced and overcame numerous changes of fortune. Two disastrous fires, two world wars, the Depression years and other economic upheavals, as well as years when the apple crop was poor. If James could return today, he would undoubtedly recognize the plant's familiar location but he would be astounded by the company's growth and development.

James, who had emigrated from England to Canada at the end of the nineteenth century, chose Trenton as the site of his cold storage plant because of its geographical location, on Lake Ontario and its potential for future growth. It was well situated in the centre of Ontario's apple country. James' refrigerated warehouse was the first to be built between Toronto and Montreal.

Trenton, situated at the mouth of the Trent River and the shores of the Bay of Quinte, had been incorporated as a village in 1853, and as a town in 1880. In 1900, the population was well under 5,000. A busy lake port, it was served by the Grand Trunk, Canadian Pacific and Central Ontario railways. These were important facilities at a time when roads were badly maintained and often impassable in the spring. Trenton had abundant waterpower and was lighted by electricity. The Trent Canal was under construction.

In those early days one could sink ankle-deep in mud while walking the streets in the spring, Most sidewalks were made of wood. One 1900 critic, in a newspaper article, speaking of proposed concrete sidewalks and good drainage, claimed "The early fathers of Trenton did nothing right." The east and west sections of the town were joined by a large, covered timber bridge.

For the past one hundred years, the history of Eben James and his descendants is closely entwined with the history and development of Trenton.

During the Second World War, when the export of apples was no longer possible, the plant was converted, as part of the war effort, to an egg storage facility where eggs were broken, processed, dried and shipped overseas. In 1945, the company found it difficult to make the transition from wartime to peacetime. The plant needed renovation, the company founder was by then in the twilight of his life, new products and customers had to be found. The company turned to vegetable freezing and storage.

At the time of the founder's death, in 1949, his son, also named Eben, was equally determined to succeed. He would successfully develop the vegetable freezing business by contracting with the Stokely Van Camp

Company, and later other companies, to freeze and store their products. Business steadily improved and, over the years, TCS grew from a modest 300,000 cubic feet to more than 12½ million cubic feet. It is now the third largest public refrigeration food warehousing and distribution business in Canada.

Eben James II founded and developed other successful businesses and persuaded many companies, mostly in the food industry, to establish their plants in Trenton.

Today, Eben James II's son, Eben W.O. James, is President and Chief Executive Officer and oversees a rapidly expanding company that confidently meets the challenges of an ever-changing marketplace in an increasingly competitive world. Unlike the first two Eben's, who controlled the company directly, the present company president chairs a leadership committee of senior management who follow the Japanese concensus-based decision model of senior management.

But one thing remains constant, a descendant of founder Eben James still heads the company.

Few 100-year-old companies remain family owned. One American business professor estimated that only about 15% of family businesses make three generations. For family businesses to both survive and thrive the management must continue to be resourceful and innovative. This Trenton Cold Storage has done.

Today, Trenton Cold Storage serves the complex logistics needs of food manufacturers and producers across North America and operates Canada's largest freight pooling and consolidation program.

This book marks the company's 100th anniversary, honours its founder, his descendants, and all those who helped to build this great enterprise. It challenges the new generation to even greater achievements. Regardless of markets, a company cannot succeed without productive, quality-conscious people who provide extraordinary customer service. These qualities TCS people have in full measure.

CHAPTER 1

The Early Years

The story of Trenton Cold Storage, in its many guises, is also the story of three generations of the James family who built and operated the company for 100 years. Its founder brought it through two world wars, the Great Depression and many other vicissitudes, including two major fires.

Ebenezer James, an Englishman, who first came to Canada in 1889 as a 16-year old boy, studied at W.H. Shaw's Central Business College in Stratford, Ont. in 1892. At the age of 28, in 1902, he founded The Apple and Produce Storage and Forwarding Company in Trenton, Ontario. It was then the first cold storage plant between Toronto and Montreal. Within a few years, James was handling over 25 per cent of all the apples exported overseas from Ontario.

Eben James I as a boy in England.

A sharp decline in ocean freight rates and the arrival of refrigerated ocean steamers had aided the export of apples overseas.

In 1902, Trenton was still a young community and the early days of its settlement were within living memory.

James was born January 2, 1874, in Loughborough, Leicestershire according to an affidavit from England found in his papers. Attempts to find his birth records have been unsuccessful and few details of his early life are known. The affidavitt, was signed by H.A. Hazelrigg, Winnifred N. Clarke and Laura Clarke, who claimed to have known him "since infancy." It declares he was born in 1874 and that his birthday was "kept on January 2nd." The Clarkes were related to his mother.

Born to Emma Wakefield, who was in ill health, Ebenezer was brought up by his great aunt, Emma Tebbutt. His father Richard's occupation, recorded on James' wedding certificate, issued in 1921, was that of "soldier." According to family lore, Richard James served in the Indian Army but few

Eben James with an aunt and cousins in England.

certain facts of his father's or Eben's early days can be found. Eben attended a boarding school at Brighton.

James began his career in the fruit industry with Woodall & Co., Temple Court, Liverpool, buying and selling apples. A memorandum dated Oct. 29, 1896 shows he was also dealing with J.R. Clogg & Co., of Montreal. Clogg was an importer and wholesale dealer in foreign and Canadian fruits and had business connections with Woodall.

A small order book, the carbon duplicate pages now difficult to decipher, reveals James was in Glasgow in the fall of 1896 where he made sales in Glasgow, Edinburgh, Aberdeen and Newcastle. A receipt from the Douglas Hotel, 17 Princes Street, Edinburgh shows he was in that city for two days at the beginning of October.

This Methodist ticket was issued in Montreal in 1894.

A Dominion Commercial Travellers' Association card, giving his address as Montreal, dated May 14, 1895 survives, as well as a YMCA, Montreal card for the same year. A letter dated Nov. 14, 1896 from J.R. Clogg & Co., Montreal to James refers to "trunks" still stored in his "old room".

A letter from Woodall and Co., dated in

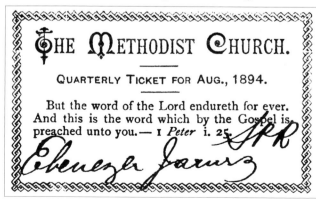

The Methodist Church.

QUARTERLY TICKET FOR AUG., 1894.

But the word of the Lord endureth for ever. And this is the word which by the Gospel is preached unto you. — I *Peter* i. 25.

Ebenezer James

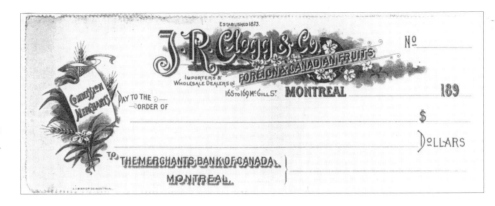

A blank cheque from the J.R. Clogg & Co. firm.

April, 1897, speaks of his return to Canada, Woodall observing he was pleased to see he had "landed all in one piece," despite having a "rough time" on the trip. He updated him on the prices received for Canadian apples, said prices for oranges had improved and that shipments of Egyptian onions had arrived in poor condition.

In 1897, James was advertising in the Glasgow *Herald*, under box number 2713, seeking to represent a whisky manufacturer in Canada. One of the replies he received expressing interest in his proposition was from Wm. Teacher & Sons Scotch Whisky Distillers, Blenders and Exporters, of Glasgow but nothing developed from this enquiry.

He was, however, appointed as Canadian agent for three large United Kingdom fruit firms in 1897: Woodall & Co., Liverpool; Boyd Barrow & Co., Glasgow; and M. Isaacs & Sons, London. Woodall was the largest exporter of Canadian apples at that time and may have been the first company to import Canadian apples into the United Kingdom. James spent one season in Montreal before moving to the old Board of Trade Building in Toronto and then to an office at 103 Union Station.

Woodall's letter appointing James as a Canadian agent commencing with the 1897-98 apple crop is dated Feb. 12, 1897 and is addressed to James in Glasgow. The commission was set at two and a half per cent with an annual guarantee of £200 "to include your office expenses, travelling, postages, cables and other expenses." James also had to post a £1000 bond, confirming the fact that the relatives who had brought him up were relatively wealthy.

Travelling between Toronto and Montreal, James soon found Eastern Ontario was the best district for buying apples. In 1900 he found the crop in Northumberland County to be "exceptionally heavy and clean." Its central location between Toronto and Montreal on Lake Ontario, provided good shipping by both lake boat and rail. This led James to contemplate setting up his own cold storage facility in Trenton. No other place in the producing districts had such advantages for shipment by water or rail, he claimed. His head office remained in Toronto for a further 10 years, however, moving to Trenton only after he founded a cooperage business there.

The export of apples to England from this area began around 1866, according to a genealogical book of the Samuel Williams Jemima Platt family, which was privately published in 1967.

Caleb Williams early took an interest in growing apples, an industry well

Eben James was a member of the Dominion Commercial Travellers Association for decades.

established in Adolphustown by 1820. His son, John P. expanded the business and began to manufacture barrels in a former fruit-house where the packing also took place.

Northern Spies, Russets, St. Lawrence, Talman, Green Sweets and Snow apples were grown. "By 1866 two paddle-wheel steamers came to Picton Harbour and probably about this time, John P. arranged to send a trial shipment of apples to England. This was the first shipment from Ontario (John P. always claimed) and he was required to guarantee the freight. And so began a most profitable export trade for the Williams family and for Ontario."

David McAuley of North Marysburgh, an immigrant from Ireland, who died Jan. 19, 1873, was, according to *Pioneer Life on the Bay of Quinte* (the original publication date is unknown but is likely about 1905) was one of the first buyers in Prince Edward County to ship apples to Montreal and Quebec.

"While in partnership with A.C. Dulmage, David McAuley became the first shipper of apples from the Bay of Quinte to England and it was largely due to his intelligent foresight that the export trade was opened up to Prince Edward County. His first consignment to the Old Country consisted of two thousand barrels."

Trenton at the turn of the century was a prosperous community. Growing from a settlement known as Trent Port, at the mouth of the Trent River, it was incorporated as the village of Trenton in 1853 and as a town on Dominion Day, 1880, with the new Mayor and Council taking office in January, 1881. The citizens celebrated and evergreen arches were constructed across the streets and shop fronts and windows were decorated with evergreen, flags and bunting. So many spruce, hemlock and cedar trees and branches were placed along the streets that "it was like walking through a forest to promenade through the principle streets of Trenton," reported *The Intelligencer* of Belleville. On Jan. 1, 1881, Dr. H.W. Day took office as the town's first mayor.

The population, as recorded in the 1901 Census, was 4,215. It was the junction point of the Grand Trunk Railway and the local Central Ontario Railway. The Murray Canal had opened navigation between the Bay of Quinte and Lake Ontario. Trenton was later a Divisional Point for the Canadian

The Alexandria loaded with barrels of apples in Picton harbour.

Northern Railway. Steamships connected Trenton with lake ports in both Canada and the United States and, of particular interest to James, to Montreal from where apples could be shipped directly to England.

In 1897, the Laurier Government had funded cold storage rooms in Canadian vessels in order to develop the lucrative United Kingdom trade in fruit and cheese. Instead of expenditures on cold storage, commented the editor of the Trenton *Courier* during an election campaign, "(Sir Charles) Tupper wants to spend millions of the people's money on a fast steamship line – a notion that we should not tolerate."

Speaking at a Liberal Rally in October, 1900, Robert Fraser of Trenton (James' future father-in-law) said cold storage on ships was now "so perfected that pears, peaches and other fine fruit were landed in England in perfect condition." Laurier and his Liberals easily won the 1900 general election.

The town was prosperous and Trenton Customs returns show exports for December, 1899 had been $32,980 and exports for the past quarter had totalled $70,051.

Local steamships included the Steamer *Varuna*, Capt. Alfred Hicks; the Steamer *North King*, and the *Ella Ross*, under Capt. D. B. Christie. The *Alexandria* shipped "enormous loads" of apples, cheese, canned goods and miscellaneous freight to Montreal.

The *Courier*, a lively newspaper published in the town since December, 1866, claimed Northumberland County was the biggest apple producer in Ontario, having over 336,000 apple trees of 15 years and over.

Trenton had many and varied industries and these had been attracted by offering the promoters municipal bonuses to establish their factories in town, a practice carried out by most cities and towns and encouraged by the province at that time.

The newspapers at the turn of the century were full of stories on the South

7

Eben James in his Toronto office, 1901.

African War. The *Courier* reported on the burning of an effigy of Kruger in Trenton when the townsfolk learned of the Relief of Ladysmith. The effigy of Kruger, "fixed up by Trenton boys, was a sturdy looking chap of immense size reared on a high pole with a broad brimmed hat sufficient to shade him from the African sun." A number of Trenton and area men had gone overseas with Canada's Second Contingent.

The report of Chief of Police T.H. Coleman for 1899, published in January, 1900, revealed many incidents of drunk and disorderly behavior in town. Some 311 tramps had sought protection and overnight lodging in the cells during the year. Gambling was also a problem. Editor George Young, M.A., described the gamblers as "the burrs, thistles and warts of human nature," and said the police should be severely reprimanded for their neglect of duty in failing to deal with the gambling problem.

A citizen, who identified himself as "Property Owner" in a letter to the editor complained of the lack of enforcement of the cow bylaw; he observed it was not a pleasant thing for a citizen to graze his cattle on the highway "and make a barnyard of the streets."

Frequent fires had also posed many problems for the town and another letter writer spoke of the remains of burned buildings left standing for months, and sometimes for many years, "a disgrace to our town and is so regarded by visitors to Trenton."

"Granolithic" sidewalks were, however, beginning to replace the wooden sidewalks in town much to the delight of the merchants and citizens, even though one sceptic, said "the early fathers of Trenton did nothing right." He felt no cement sidewalks should be constructed until a proper system of drainage had been developed.

The town also boasted of the availability of electricity, "during the day as well as at night." The first electric arc lamps had been installed on downtown streets in 1886.

Automobiles were rarely seen, however, and one such carriage, a Gladstone, "the wheels rubber tired," passed through Trenton in October, 1900 "swiftly and noiselessly," causing "quite an attraction."

A lengthy story on Eben James appears in the June 6th, 1901 edition of the *Courier*. James, described as a Toronto apple exporter, had recently returned from a trip to California where he had visited the "Newton Pippin district" and had been "very much struck with the extreme care which the American growers take in their orchards."

"As one of the largest receivers of apples for export, and, therefore, having the interests of the Canadian growers very much at heart, I could not but compare these well-kept orchards with many of our own."

The Ontario orchards did not compare well at all, he said. Many farmers regarding their orchards as of little value and took little care with pruning and cultivation. In fact, he said, "Canada can, on account of its northern location, grow better keeping apples than most sections of the United States but care must be taken to produce quality apples for export."

"An orchard cannot produce good fruit without proper care any more than a cow can produce milk without food." A good apple crop, James claimed, can pay as well as any other crop a farmer can grow. Consideration should also be given to growing the most marketable varieties. He recommended Baldwin, King, Greening, Russet and Canada Red, noting the Spy is a Canadian apple that only attains its best here in this country.

An Act for the marking and inspection of fruit to prevent fraudulent packing was passed in September at the last session of Parliament, to come into

.. THE ..

Apple *and* Produce

COLD STORAGE

AND

Forwarding Co., Limited

Incorporated by the Dominion Government
under "The Companies Act, 1902"

CAPITAL:

Stock Authorized, One Hundred Thousand Dollars

OFFICERS AND DIRECTORS:

HY. PEDWELL, President
Lumber Merchant, Mill Owner and Fruit Exporter, Thornbury

EBEN JAMES, Manager
Apple Exporter and Receiver's Agent, Toronto

MILTON PEDWELL, Secretary-Treasurer

MONTGOMERY, FLEURY & MONTGOMERY, Solicitors, Toronto

DIRECTORS:

HY. PEDWELL, Thornbury	DAVID GREGG, London, Eng.
EBEN JAMES, Toronto	JNO. HARE, " "
W. R. DEMPSEY, Albury	JOHN A. HARE, " "
ALFRED WOODALL, Liverpool, Eng.	

EXECUTIVE COMMITTEE:

H. PEDWELL   EBEN JAMES   W. R. DEMPSEY

The title page of James' Cold Storage Prospectus.

Share Certificate 1902.

effect on July 1, 1902. Closed packages and barrels of fruit would have to be marked with the full surname and initials of first names and the address of the packer as well as with the variety of the fruit and grade. Failure to comply or the use of false markings would bring penalties to the packers. The local apple inspector, Elmer Lick of Oshawa, held meetings to make the new regulations known to growers.

James and other apple buyers found an apple famine in the fall of 1901. Poor spring weather had affected the yield locally. However, W.H. Dempsey of Trenton received a gold medal at the Pan-American Exposition in Buffalo, N.Y. for his display of apples while W.M. Warner of Trenton received an honorable mention. Sponsored by the state and federal governments the exposition was intended to celebrate the accomplishments of the 19th century.

The Brighton *Ensign* of Feb. 7, 1902 reported Capt. Alfred Hicks had built a new dry dock at Trenton. Men and teams of horses were employed to cut the way clear so that the steamer *Varuna* could be put in the new dock.

Eben James wrote a letter calling for better care of orchards that was published in the April 11, edition of the Brighton *Ensign*. "Much is being done by the Government in the way of improving transportation and enacting stringent laws to compel dealers to pack honestly, but unless the grower produces the required quality these facilities and stringent regulations will be of little value."

Improved methods of cold storage now make it possible for growers in Missouri, Arkansas and other "warm States" to store their apples, James wrote, bringing more competition to Ontario farmers. Poor quality apples cannot be handled at a profit, while good fruit will do very well. Eastern Ontario apples, including those from Prince Edward County, as well as those grown in the Niagara District are of good quality while other districts are "in a deplorable state".

James issued a handsome prospectus offering shares in The Apple and Produce Storage and Forwarding Co'y. Henry Pedwell of Thornbury, Ont., was President and James manager. James had made the acquaintance of Pedwell during his apple-buying travels and had interested him in investing in his new company. Pedwell was a lumber merchant, mill owner and fruit exporter. He had also been a member of the first Thornbury Council in 1887 and mayor in 1899-1900.

The Apple & Produce Cold Storage & Forwarding Co.

Abbreviation
A.P.C.S.&F.Co.
Limited

Storage at Trenton,
Western Office,
703 Board of Trade Bldg., Toronto

EBEN JAMES, MANAGER

Trenton, Dec., 4th., 1902.

I hereby appoint, (Eben James) proxy, for me and in my place, and at our general meeting of The Apple & Produce Cold Storage & Forwarding Co., Ltd., and in respect to myself in said Company, on all questions submitted at such meeting and act for me there as fully and effectually as myself personally.

A proxy from W.R. Dempsey giving Eben James voting rights.

Pedwell was born in Wales in 1849 and emigrated to Pennsylvania in 1870. After a few months in the U.S.A. he moved to Collingwood where he took up the trade of machinest blacksmith. Later he moved to Thornbury where he started in the blacksmithing and carriage business. He later swapped this business for a sawmill which he ran for many years. In time he became a very rich man, building a large residence at the corner of Bruce Street and Alice Streets in 1900. He also built "the Pedwell block," as it was known, the old bank building, on the corner of Bruce and Arthur Streets, in Thornbury.

Company officers were Eben James, Managing Director, listed as an apple exporter and receiver's agent, Toronto; Milton Pedwell, secretary-treasurer (who was one of Hy. Pedwell's sons), and Montgomery, Fleury & Montgomery, solicitors, Toronto. Directors were: Henry Pedwell, Eben James, W.R. Dempsey, Albury; Alfred Woodall, Liverpool, England, David Gregg, London, England, Jno. Hare, and John A. Hare, both of London, England.

The executive committee was made up of Henry Pedwell, Eben James and W.R. Dempsey. The company was incorporated under the Companies Act, 1902 and the authorized stock capital was to be $100,000. Shares were $100 each and the *Courier* editor said several "of our shrewd apple men have invested and the building half built has been used to its utmost capacity this winter. All speak highly of its success."

The cold storage, which was located on one and a three-quarter acres of land, would handle apples, cheese and other farm produce, including poultry.

The solid stone building was to be four stories high but owing to the lateness of the season when work was started only two stories were completed in the first year of operation. This permitted 25,000 barrels of apples to be stored and forwarded by rail and water for overseas.

Henry Pedwell

South view of dock showing deep water channel and foundation of Cold Storage Warehouse and private dock, 1902.

The Apple and Produce Cold Storage and Forwarding Company was kept busy during the winter months employing an average of 25 men, picking over apples, re-sorting and re-packing for overseas shipment. They averaged 10 rail cars a week, each car having a capacity of 150 barrels. Most of the barrels were shipped to the London and Liverpool markets. In addition to providing employment the company gave business to steamers, barges and railroads and provided a new dock for the large lake steamers.

James had been in Trenton early in February, 1903 contracting for stone to complete his cold storage warehouse. Tenders were let for drawing stone from the area of the Central Ontario Railway gravel pit by rail to the cold storage building. Arrangements were made to install the British Linde System of refrigeration as well as other machinery.

The *Courier* for Feb. 19 reported Mark Lee of Brighton had been appointed to a position in the apple packing department of the cold storage warehouse. J.D. Gilbert of Picton was also employed in the storage during the winter and, on his return to Picton, could not speak too highly of the cold storage system, said *The Picton Gazette*.

The annual meeting of the Company was held at 703, Board of Trade Building, Toronto on Monday, Feb. 23 when preparations were made for the completion of the top floors of the cold storage building.

Mayor Jesse Funnell and Councillor T.A. O'Rourke were in Toronto securing the patent from the Crown necessary for the transfer of town owned lands to the Cold Storage as well as the adjoining Marine Ways lands.

Eben James was back in England in March, returning in mid-April to Canada on the *Tunisian*.

In April, the cold storage company planked all the space from the building out to the pier and erected a storehouse for freight. A road from the post office to the dock was constructed. The water depth at the wharf was over 10 feet.

In May, Mr. Ward, the member for East Durham, in arguing the merits of Port Hope over Trenton as the future terminus of the Trent Canal, said the water depth in Trenton was only seven feet, while Port Hope's harbor was 10 feet. James retorted that the Cold Storage Co., had only to build a wharf of sufficient width outside their building to secure over 10 feet of water and that, without dredging, Trenton's river was from 10 to 13 feet deep.

James was active in the Trenton Board of Trade and at the May, 1903 meeting was one of four people nominated as president. Dr. W.S. Jaques was acclaimed to office after the others declined their nominations. James and Robert Fraser were named to the board's council.

In June, James proposed to lay down a second railway track to the cold storage building but ran into opposition from his neighbour, Capt. Alfred Hicks of the Marine Railway and Shipyards who claimed that he would be trespassing on his property.

Editor Young expressed concern about the dispute as many skilled mechanics were employed at the Marine Railway. "There is," he declared, "no institution in Trenton outside of Gilmour's Factory and Mills of so much importance to Trenton. This business is yet in its infancy and more ground is already wanted to accommodate the men working on the boats."

If they had three ways ready, "a thing they are constantly aiming at," said Young, they would all be occupied before this in the repairing of boats. He said the merchants appreciated the ready cash paid to the Marine Railway employees each week, "and we are glad they stood by the Captain in this matter."

James, who had been away in Montreal at the time of the complaint, may have had a few words with the editor for the next issue carried a complimentary paragraph about his warehouse: "The Cold Storage building is nearing completion and will be a fine substantial one. The new wharf and the other improvements in progress on the waterfront, add greatly to the appearance and the convenience of the harbor."

A letter from James appeared in the July 2 edition of the newspaper stating that the proposed railway track would be completely on land owned by the cold storage company. "There is plenty of room." He criticized the editor's remarks that had appeared under the heading "A Breeze".

Under the heading "Night work," the *Courier* reported some men had been employed laying rails for the second track into the cold storage building. "This is evidently the beginning of trouble," he wrote. "It appears to us the second track could be laid down close to the stone building and a common roadway where the attempt is made to lay the second track. Capt. Hicks says if this strip is taken from him he will go to Belleville where he is offered encouragement. We hope Council may be able to reconcile the differences."

Council sided with Eben James in the dispute over the ownership of the land and Capt. Hicks was incensed. He immediately put advertisements in the local newspapers headed "Shipways for Sale,"

"The Marine Shipways in the Town of Trenton in good condition will be sold at cost. A large barge on the ways for repairs will be turned over to the purchaser. Apply to Capt. Hicks, Trenton, July 16th, 1903."

Meanwhile, said the editor, the council was doing what it could to harmonize the dispute between James and Captain Hicks. Despite his threat to move, Capt. Hicks remained in Trenton operating the shipways for many more years.

In July, the first refrigeration equipment "to manufacture the cold" arrived at the cold storage building.

In August, the newspaper again reported James had been on a business trip to Montreal.

In mid-August the cold storage had a Mr. Wilkinson and his two sons from New York and Buffalo working at the warehouse, putting it "in first class condition." This work entailed installing five dead air sections between each storey and the outside walls. The foundations for the machinery were built and, the *Courier* reported, "a houseful of piping is piled on the dock."

Wilkinson, who designed and installed cold storage plants, had previously fitted up one in Japan and another in Australia.

"When completed, Trenton will have a first class article, none superior in Canada," said the newspaper. "Mr. Wilkinson is enthusiastic over our town and its natural utilities. If they had such a town, of such power facilities in the States, it would have a population of 200,000."

Gilmour's Saw Mill had shut down for four weeks because of the lack of saw logs and a number of their employees found temporary work at the cold storage building.

Sailing was one of Eben James pleasures and the Aug. 27 edition of the *Courier* records the sale of his yacht "*Gipsy*" to Gershom Bonter.

In September, the Cobourg *Sentinel-Star* said D. Taylor of Trenton was in Cobourg buying apples to be stored at the Cold Storage Co. in Trenton. The newspaper said this was one of the finest buildings in Ontario with a capacity of 60,000 barrels, "and has railways connections with several lines at the dock."

Cold storage was catching on with many farmers and R. J. Graham of the Farmers' Association said 10 farmers were looking for cold storage facilities this year compared to one last year. He said all available cold storage space on ocean ships had been booked months ahead.

Forty-two thousand barrels of Canadian apples were reported on their way to the London market, "record prices being assured."

In November, 1903, Harry Dempsey of Rednerville (as it was spelled at that time) advertised for rooms for light housekeeping within a short distance of the cold storage warehouse. He was engaged for some time repacking his apples at the plant.

By February, 1904, James had about 50 hands engaged in re-packing apples for export at the cold storage, although Trenton was, that winter, suffering from heavy snow falls which were causing train delays, and coal shortages. Many people were ill with "La Grippe" (influenza).

CHAPTER 2

Destroyed by Fire

Fire destroyed the cold storage warehouse owned by the Apple and Produce Storage and Forwarding Company Limited early Saturday morning, Feb. 20, 1904. The entire contents, including the recently installed machinery were lost.

When the fire brigade arrived about 1 a.m. the interior was burning fiercely and the flames had made considerable headway. All efforts to save the building were futile but the firemen were able to save the property adjoining.

Nothing but the bare walls of the cold storage, which had only been completed the previous fall, were left standing. The building had been 124 feet long by 94 feet wide, four stories high and built of local stone.

The company had a capital stock of $100,000, reported the *Courier*. Company president was Henry Pedwell, of Thornbury; Eben James, manager; Milton Pedwell, secretary-treasurer; and W.R. Dempsey, a former member of provincial parliament, of Prince Edward County were directors.

The building had been fitted with the Linde British system of refrigeration, run by a 50-horse power electric motor. Some 12,000 barrels of apples had been stored in the building and the total loss on fruit and machinery was estimated at $60,000, this amount being partially covered by insurance.

"The explosions that were occasionally heard during the fire were caused by the bursting of large iron cylinders containing ammonia," the *Courier* said. "There were twelve of these cylinders, each ten feet long. Six car loads of apples were ready for shipment the next day."

Trenton town council held a special meeting on Monday evening to see what help could be offered to encourage the company to rebuild the plant, "and to consider the propriety of entering into some new and reasonable arrangement to encourage the rebuilding of the said storage property and other matters."

James and his solicitor, J.D. Montgomery, attended the special session and said the company hoped to rebuild the plant immediately, at the same time enlarging the facility, and requested council to consider an exemption from municipal taxes for 10 years. Council agreed in principle to this request and referred the matter to the industrial commission for study "to deal with as though the whole council were acting."

Present at the council meeting were Mayor Jesse Funnell and Councillors W.J. Preston, W.H. Matthews, P.J. O'Rourke, Jas. Shurie and G.A. White.

The Cold Storage in Trenton was destroyed by fire on Feb. 20, 1904.

Following the council meeting James left for Toronto to meet with the company directors. Later in the week, James, lawyer J.D. Montgomery and Hy. Pedwell, spent a few days in Trenton inspecting the damaged building.

Council met again on March 21 in special session to look at the Cold Storage request. Council agreed to modify the original agreement after they learned insurance claims had been settled and that the Company had decided to rebuild as soon as weather permitted. James decided to add an additional 100 square feet of space.

An article in an industrial section of the *Courier*, published on April, 7 1904, and presumably written before the Cold Storage fire, spoke of the town's industrial development. The writer referred to the big saw mill of Gilmour & Company, Ltd., "with its towering smokestack, conceded to be at the time of its erection, the largest saw mill on the American Continent and the large stone structure of the Apple and Produce Cold Storage and Forwarding Company, Ltd., the works of the Canadian Canners' Consolidated Co., Ltd., and the Shipyard (which) combine to give the town an important business aspect."

The article, entitled The Busy Town of Trenton, said "...Trenton's fire protection is so efficient that a real serious fire is an unknown event in the recent history of the town. The town has an excellent fire department, a powerful fire engine, a good fire alarm system and firemen of the right calibre."

On May 26, the newspaper reported Eben James of Toronto was in town and was shortly on his way to England, presumably to report on the fire loss to the British shareholders.

James' returned from England late in June. He was expected to arrive in Trenton with plans for the rebuilding of the warehouse. "We are all anxious to see the rebuilding commenced at once," said the *Courier*.

Prior to the loss of the cold storage building, John E. Terrill of Trenton, had, in the previous fall, tried his own storage methods for apples. He had buried several barrels of apples as an experiment and in the Spring when they were dug up he found them to be "in splendid condition." This method had considerable risks, however, observed the editor. An Attica, N.Y., farmer, Edward Nevinger, had buried 140 barrels of apples to preserve them but when he dug them up he got only 20 barrels of good fruit.

On July 4, council met to consider a bylaw exempting the Apple and Produce Cold Storage and Forwarding Company, Ltd., from taxation (except school taxes) for a period of 10 years. At the same time the yearly $500 bonus against taxes that had been allowed in the agreement when the warehouse had first been constructed was cancelled.

In addition to the bonus arrangement in the original agreement town council had provided the building site to the company.

The exemption from taxes in the new bylaw was to apply to the building and future additions as well as the lands, plant and machinery but not to the wharf or dock part of the property. The agreement was subject to the company rebuilding the warehouse in substantially the same size as the one destroyed by fire and to employ from 25 to 50 hands during the packing season each year during the 10 years of the agreement. The new building was to be erected within a year from the passing of the bylaw.

Before the new bylaw could be implemented it had to be passed by a vote of the ratepayers of the municipality and this vote was set for Monday, Aug. 1, 1904.

At the same meeting council also discussed a bylaw to provide a loan of $20,000 to the Ontario Electric Railway. The ratepayers would also vote on this proposal.

The *Courier* encouraged the ratepayers to vote in favor of the two money bylaws. The editor reviewed the original bylaw for the Cold Storage that had provided for a free site, exemption for taxes for five years and a $500 yearly bonus.

"The building and outlay have been a great benefit to Trenton costing the town practically nothing and has been filled to its capacity during the two years of operation. During the winter months it has paid out as high as $500 per week for wages all spent in Trenton. The building brings business from western parts of Ontario which otherwise would not come to Trenton. Should the Co. not rebuild it may be hard to get a private individual to take hold of the property and run it to its utmost capacity as in the past, as to operate successfully an institution of that size it needs a firm behind it with a large export business. The building is at present an eye-sore and the sooner it is rebuilt the better for the town. Vote for the Cold Storage By-Law."

James took a day off at the end of July. The newspaper reported he had been fishing at Consecon.

A three-fifths majority was required to pass the bylaws and both passed easily on August 1. Some 363 voted for the Cold Storage bylaw with 49 against, while 339 voted for the Ontario Electric Railway loan with 74 opposed. Council passed the bylaws early in September.

James left for Toronto the day after the vote and also visited the World's Fair at St. Louis.

Work commenced immediately. On Aug. 11, the newspaper reported "Eben James with his characteristic energy has had a channel dredged out at the east side of the Cold Storage wharf by the Weddell Dredging Co's dredge 'Trenton'. The rock dredged out was used to make a solid filling for the wharf."

"We understand the dredging will be continued along the east side of the building. The rock will be utilized to build a roadway on that side besides the advantage of having a channel for boats."

The *Courier* said about 40 men were engaged in the work. "The activity down at the water front reminds us of last year. A gang of men are repairing the railway switch, Captain Hicks has men filling in at the ways, and men are actively engaged in rebuilding the Cold Storage with the intention of having it roofed in for this season's apple crop."

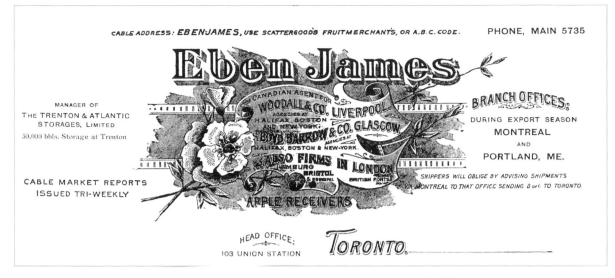

CABLE ADDRESS: EBENJAMES, USE SCATTERGOOD'S FRUITMERCHANTS, OR A.B.C. CODE.   PHONE, MAIN 5735

Eben James

MANAGER OF
THE TRENTON & ATLANTIC
STORAGES, LIMITED
50,000 bbls. Storage at Trenton

CANADIAN AGENT FOR
WOODALL & CO. LIVERPOOL
AGENCIES AT
HALIFAX BOSTON
AND NEW YORK;
BOYD BARROW & CO. GLASCOW
AGENCIES AT
HALIFAX, BOSTON & NEW-YORK.

ALSO FIRMS IN LONDON
HAMBURG
BRISTOL
& BREMEN.   BRITISH PORTS.

CABLE MARKET REPORTS
ISSUED TRI-WEEKLY

APPLE RECEIVERS

BRANCH OFFICES,
DURING EXPORT SEASON
MONTREAL
AND
PORTLAND, ME.

SHIPPERS WILL OBLIGE BY ADVISING SHIPMENTS
VIA MONTREAL TO THAT OFFICE SENDING B or L. TO TORONTO.

HEAD OFFICE:
103 UNION STATION   TORONTO.

An electric motor was installed at the warehouse and by the end of September the *Courier* said "the fourth story is nearly completed and the roof will shortly be put on." Fifteen carpenters and their helpers were working on the roof and apples for storage were expected as soon as the building was ready in October.

Trenton citizens had been entertained by a balloon ascension from Victoria Park, Trenton in August. "Judging by the crowd which assembled, the interest in these events increases," said the *Courier*. "The preliminaries were watched with intense interest, and as the intrepid Prof. Stewart left terra firma everybody cheered."

The social column for Sept. 22, 1904, noted Col. Hendricks and Mr. Dougall, of Belleville, were guests of Eben James at "The Grove".

More activity was taking place at the waterfront with Capt. Hicks employing a gang of men working on the shipways.

Buyers were offering 50¢ per barrel for fall apples, and 75¢ a barrel for winter fruit. "When the farmer has to board the pickers and draw the apples to the station there is very little profit, in fact, it hardly pays to bother with fall apples at the prices offered," said the *Courier*.

The Ontario crop was not nearly as large as a year earlier, said the *Canadian Horticulturist*, and claimed growers should be receiving better prices than have been offered. "Growers should not accept less than 75¢ to $1.00 per barrel on the trees…"

A week later, the *Courier* was reporting heavy winds had caused considerable damage to the area apple crops, "In the majority of orchards half the apples are on the ground."

Early in November, large numbers of apples arrived at the Cold Storage building. A new high-level freight shed was built on the wharf replacing an existing shed. The new shed, 40 x 80 foot, was built at the edge of the wharf instead of against the cold storage building as previously.

The *Courier* predicted the coming of the Standard Chemical Company to Trenton, "almost a settled matter" and said the company planned to erect a $150,000 factory on the Gilmour & Co. property.

An early letterhead listing firms represented by Eben James.

Fire again struck the town three days before Christmas when Forbes basket factory, a frame building, full of inflammable material, on the bay shore near the C.O.R. station was destroyed.

Mayor Jesse Funnell, who had served for three years, retired from council in January, 1905 and was succeeded by former mayor W.S. Jaques.

The winter produced fierce blizzards and heavy snowfalls and roads were often impossible for teams to travel. One February blizzard lasted 36 hours and Central Ontario Railway mail trains to Wellington were cancelled.

In February, the recently formed Ontario Fruit Growers' Association said they would make representations to the Ontario government asking that the Act passed five years earlier providing grants for establishing cold storage facilities be extended for a further five years. The original act was due to expire in March, 1905. The association also asked that aid be extended to the central shipping stations. One of the association's vice-presidents was W.H. Dempsey of Trenton.

The weekly *Sun,* another newspaper published in Trenton, commented on recent shipments of Nova Scotia apples to Great Britain by a sailing vessel. The vessel which carried the apples was named the *Skoda*, and reached London on Jan. 2, after a stormy passage of 23 days. Surprisingly, the cargo, on the whole, was in good condition although a few barrels of apples were somewhat "wasty."

The annual report of the Chief of Police revealed the usual parade of drunk and disorderly persons, the arrest of two "incorrigible girls" as well as six charges for violation of the fruit act.

In March, 1905, James left for a business trip to South Africa where he was to look into the export of apples and other fruits. He returned from South Africa via England spending two months in England, Scotland, Ireland and other European countries.

James was back in town by June and, at this time, was referred to in the

This cornercard included the company's lengthy name and its abbreviated form.

newspapers as the general manager of the Trenton and Atlantic Storages, Ltd., the new name adopted by the company after the rebuilding.

In early April, W.J. Pringle and C. Driscoll had been awarded the contract for the carpentry work to be undertaken at the Cold Storage and this work was completed by the end of May.

A crop report prepared by J.A. Aitken for the Toronto *Globe* predicted a heavy apple yield for Northumberland County in the fall of 1905, particularly in the area from Colborne to Trenton, and anticipated a large quantity being stored in the cold storage facilities.

The 1903 apple yield in Northumberland had been estimated at 2,465,000 bushels and at 2,911,000 bushels in 1904. The 1905 crop was expected to be larger because of high yield and increased acreage. The number of Spy apples was decreasing while more Stark variety apples were being grown, in addition to Ben Davis, Greenings, Pippins and Russets.

Edward H. Woodall, of the Liverpool firm of Woodall & Co., one of the companies Eben James represented, was in Toronto in August. Accompanied by James, he looked at various orchards in Eastern Ontario. Woodall said his firm had bought fruit from the Hudson River country as long ago as 1847. They were included in the six great firms who auctioned 90 per cent of all the fruit imported into Liverpool, which, he said, was the largest fruit distributing centre in the world.

Woodall, who was described by the *Courier* as "probably the largest apple receiver in England," spent some time in Trenton and inspected many local orchards.

James was predicting a lighter apple crop in 1905 but one of good quality. The Baldwin variety was light, but Ben Davis and Russets were "well loaded." He said the English crop was likely to be poor with Germany, Holland and Belgium reporting light crops presenting good sales opportunities for Ontario farmers.

C.A. Nugent of Trenton, who had had connections with Trenton Cold Storage for many years, took a gang of men to Wellington in August to pack apples for the storage.

Capt. Hicks, and J. E. Rathbun were carrying out work at the shipways adjacent to the cold storage building, rebuilding portions of the ways in oak and maple, "in the best possible manner," and revitalizing the yards.

James, still referred to as "of Toronto" in the local newspapers, was in Trenton at the end of October supervising the elevation of the railway track that ran alongside the storage building to enable cars to be loaded and unloaded at the second store level.

Many apple buyers were working in the area including five in Trenton from Paris, France. A week later another buyer from Paris was in town.

By the start of November the cold storage was "taxed to the utmost" in receiving and storing apples. "Besides the apples brought in by teams," reported the *Courier*, "6 to 8 carloads are delivered daily. On Saturday last, 24 cars were waiting to be unloaded. The Colborne warehouses have been filled and the surplus has been shipped to Trenton."

Banner on Main Street, Trenton, advertises the "Bird Man".

In fact, R. and J. Coyle, who were connected with the Colborne warehouse had to send over 5,000 barrels to Trenton for storage.

James spent some weeks in Trenton in November and the newspaper noted his "knack of noticing possible improvements and (he) not only notices them but promptly puts them into execution. The elevated railway has been extended to the end of the wharf so now five cars can be accommodated instead of three. A tramway has also been built so that apple barrels can be rolled down from the Cold Storage to the boat. The dock at the south end is being extended some 30 feet."

Inside the Cold Storage a large number of hands were repacking apples, several loaded cars leaving every day. "The shipments are chiefly to England although some large consignments of Kings and Russets have been shipped to Paris, France."

As winter approached Weddell's dredge "*Trenton*" arrived in port from Northport and was being prepared for winter storage. Capt. Hall's steam barge "*Iona*" and the barge "*Ralph T. Holcomb*" were to winter at the Cold Storage dock and other craft, including the *Varuna*, were drawn up on the shipways where a new boat was to be built over the winter for the Toronto Ferry Board.

CHAPTER 3

Still Very British

The St. Andrew's Society annual dinner held at the Gilbert House in Trenton on Thursday, Nov. 30, 1905, was well attended. President Robert Weddell was in the chair and Eben James represented the St. George's Society.

James, B.H. Siddall and J.H. Campbell were each asked to respond to the toast "Commercial interests," and James predicted Canada was on the eve of the greatest development ever known. The possibilities for Canada were unlimited, he said, and Canada was becoming "the world's granary." James said he had travelled all over the world and was favorably impressed with Trenton's natural advantages.

"The Cold Storage is now employing 60 men and I believe Trenton to be the second largest apple storage centre in Canada."

Dominion fruit inspector P.J. Carey was in Trenton in late December and inspected the warehouse where Robert Coyle Sr., was packing apples under the Coyle and Peterson brand name. The inspector examined a few barrels and found them wrongly graded. The inspector left for dinner and, on his return, found the apples had been placed on a railcar and that an engine was being attached ready to haul the car away. Inspector Carey insisted on the car being held while he continued his investigation and he found that "fruit marked No. 1 was little better than trash," said the *Courier*.

Mr. Coyle was required to sign a declaration admitting that the 50 barrels in the car were all of the same grade and he was told an "information" would be laid under the Fruit Marks Act.

Woodall & Co's advices to Eben James said Canadian apples were selling in England much above the level of American apples. The Canadian King variety had fetched 26s.6d. while King apples from Maine fetched 20s.6d. a barrel. The American barrel was smaller than the Canadian barrel but the difference in size did not account for the differences in prices obtained. Most popular apples sold in Liverpool were Canadian Talman Sweet, Ben Davis, Snows, Baldwins, Greenings, Russets, Spies, and Kings.

The Brighton *Ensign*, in January, 1906, said apples purchased by the buyer P.W. Duncan, from Robert Snetsinger and J.E. McDonald had been exported to Germany where they had been sold for 32 marks a barrel, or about $7.70 Canadian. "This is a pretty good showing for Canadian Apples."

A report published in the Feb. 2, 1906 *Ensign* said the 1905 apple season had been "one of the most successful in the history of the apple trade of

The Gilbert House,
Trenton, from "The
Evolution of Trenton".

Canada." The output was not as high as in 1903, the total yield being some 800,000 barrels less, but the fruit had obtained uniformly high prices in the British market.

"From all American and Canadian ports to all ports in Great Britain the shipments for the year 1903, closing on Dec. 26, were 1,666,792 barrels. In 1904, they were 1,475,760 barrels, and in 1905, which was accepted as a record year, 2,162,558."

In March, Messrs. Farewell and Clifford shipped 300 cases of fancy Canadian apples from Trenton to Nice, Italy, where they were to be shown at an exhibition there.

In April, Hugh Ross of Meyersburg produced very fine quality Spies and, at the recommendation of his packer, he sent a barrel of the choicest to His Majesty the King as a gift. Lord Stewart, the Master of the King's Household, wrote from Buckingham Palace acknowledging, with thanks, receipt of the apples.

Area apple growers met at the Opera House, Brighton during the month and formed a local fruit growers' association. A committee was formed to look into the formation of a co-operative association.

In May, the *Ensign* reported W.H. Matthews of Trenton intended to erect a barrel factory, near the Grand Trunk station at Colborne. At the same time, the Dominion Department of Agriculture was holding meetings in fruit growing areas showing growers how to properly pack apples in boxes. The western growers were using boxes rather than barrels and had been enjoying higher prices for their produce.

British apple market prices were cabled to Eben James.

Record apple crops had been harvested in the two previous years but the 1906 crop was expected to be below average. The U.S. apple crop was expected to be high, however, "trees being loaded beyond description," according to buyer G.H. Fowler.

Eben James was not the exclusive agent for the British companies he was shipping to at this time. Apple buyer Fred C. Fiddick of Brighton was also advertising for apples to be shipped to Woodall & Co., of Liverpool, Boyd Barrow & Co., of Glasgow and M. Isaacs & Sons of London.

A lengthy article, published in the Toronto *Mail and Empire*, and reprinted in the *Ensign*, called upon the government to establish a chain of cold storage warehouses in fruit growing areas. Involved in the proposal was R.J. Cochrane, son of E. Cochrane, M.P., of Brighton. Of the estimated 17,000,000 barrels of apples produced in Canada, only 1,500,000 barrels were exported and much of the apple crop was wasted. Many farmers looked upon orchards as a sideline, the writer said, and most of the apples grown in Ontario were fed to hogs or just wasted.

"The creameries were necessary to make the cows pay, and with cold storage the apple trees of Ontario will lift a mortgage."

Initially, the Dominion Minister of Agriculture, Sydney Fisher, was interested in the proposal. On reflection, he told the House of Commons, such a scheme managed by one great corporation could lead to a monopoly in the business, "and I think the public interest would suffer."

The government was also unwilling to guarantee the company's bonds, as requested. He said the government had, on a few occasions, guaranteed bonds for some large railway corporations, but did not want to extend this to other commercial corporations.

Mayor W.S. Jacques was re-elected to council for 1907 and councillors, elected by acclamation, were J.H. Dickey, W.J. Preston, C.L. Hawley, P.J. O'Rourke, O.E. Fortune and Peter Pomery.

The water in the river and bay was very high in January and the lower doors of the Cold Storage building had to be cemented to prevent the water coming into the building. The docks overflowed and residents along the river were inconvenienced by the high water. Some residents said the river was now higher than it had been for 30 years when it had overflowed inundating some of the lower streets in town reaching as far as Ridgeway Street.

The March 7, 1907 *Courier* said a cargo of apples from Montreal had reached Cape Town, South Africa on Dec. 4 in good condition. The fruit met with a very ready sale at highly remunerative prices for the importers, said W.T.R. Preston, acting commercial agent for Canada. Although cold storage

An early Ontario orchard.

records show some references to South Africa, including the possible purchase of oranges, few details remain to confirm whether or not James became involved in the South African trade.

In May, James was travelling in British Columbia seeking additional apples for export to England. In later years, he was to purchase large quantities of apples from this province.

The apple industry was revolutionized to some extent in 1907 by apple growers working through the newly formed Canadian Apple Exporters Limited organization. Over 80 stockholders attended the first annual meeting held in Trenton, principally from the townships of Rawdon, Sidney, Murray and Ameliasburg.

The president of the association was G.A. Snarr, the secretary-treasurer J.S. Dench and vice-president and manager Walter H. Dempsey. The government fruit inspector, P.K. Carley spoke on the work of other associations and Eben James spoke on the care of orchards. He claimed that from Ontario to the Atlantic seaboard the crop was deteriorating with the exception of a few districts. Less than 20 per cent of the apples harvested were suitable for export, yet, he said, the return from properly managed apple orchards could be greater than that achieved from wheat fields.

Apple packing early 1900's.

He warned the farmers that British Columbia was making a strong bid for some of their markets, while Tasmania (Australia) was increasing its shipments to Great Britain.

Many of the visiting growers inspected the Cold Storage premises and were impressed by the shipping arrangements.

Trenton was growing and attracting industry but not as fast as *Courier* editor Clarence Young would like. His editorials deplored the way some citizens continually criticized the town. "Give a dog a bad name and hang him, is still somewhat true with a lot of our citizens and no matter what bright reports are placed before them they will shake their heads, look wise and say it cannot be true. That they would not place one cent in anything to help along the town, that a dry rot is creeping over the place and lot more nonsense of a similar character, is their daily theme."

James had faith in his town and always looked for ways to develop it, either through his own business or by supporting new development. The population had grown 360 persons in the past year and had now reached 4,500, "considerably larger than Cobourg" and new industries were starting up even though each application to the municipality for land also sought

Barrel making in early days. This picture was taken in Prince Edward County.

bonuses or an exemption from taxes for a period of time. The latest request before council was for a grant to the promoters of a smelter that would handle ore from north Hastings brought in by the Central Ontario Railway.

So, "Hurrah for our pretty and progressive town," said the *Courier*, as it encouraged ratepayers to vote in favor of the smelter grant on June 28.

The vote did not go ahead, however. At a special meeting of town council on June 25, the promoters asked for the Smelter bylaw to be withdrawn for the present.

James was overseas again and the newspaper reported his return in July, "looking exceedingly well."

The apple crops in Ontario, Nova Scotia and British Columbia all looked promising and the Toronto *World*, in a lengthy article, warned apple growers they were losing money by selling their orchards in bulk to apple buyers. They advocated the sale of apples through co-operative societies and it is clear from the tenor of the article that it was written by someone associated with one of these societies. Various examples were given of farmers who lost money by selling to apple dealers while wide-awake farmers realized the societies were "a godsend to the farmers of our fair province."

There were, apparently, about 25 co-operative societies in Ontario in 1907, "and they are meeting with much greater success than was at first anticipated."

Not all farmers viewed the co-operatives favorably, however. The *Courier* for August 22 reports I.S. Smith of Smithfield selling his crop of winter varieties to Alex Loomis for the sum of $2,500, "the largest sale in this locality."

Fire again struck Trenton when flames raced through Jesse Funnell's barn on Balsam Street near the Market Square. It spread to the hide house and drive sheds and his large coal shed also caught fire. Morrison & Maybee's livery shed started to burn and Saylor's department store was threatened. Losses exceeded $12,000.

In another disaster, a retort at the Trenton factory of Canadian Canners Consolidated Company exploded killing George B. Graham and Louis Dube.

Weddell's new tug, the *Rob. G. Weddell* which had been built on the shipways near the cold storage plant was launched in October. The 75-foot long, 16 foot wide vessel cost $15,000.

Mr. Funnell experienced another loss in November when his evaporator on Quinte Street, at the rear of the Post office, burned to the ground. The evaporator contained a large number of apples in the process of evaporation as well as many boxes of evaporated apples awaiting shipment. The loss was estimated at $8,000.

Meanwhile, shipment of apples from the cold storage reached record figures and the barrels were carried to Montreal on the steamers *Alexandria, Niagara, Water Lily* and *Aberdeen.*

Mayor Funnell was elected to office in January, 1908 succeeding Dr. W.S. Jaques who had served three terms. In March, James spoke to council asking that the road from the C.O.R. station to the Cold Storage be improved. He also asked to be allowed to continue dredging the slip to the south of his building.

He made the first public reference to a new business he intended to establish, a hoop and saw mill on the McMurchy property and he asked for riparian rights to certain water lots in front of his property. His request was referred to the Harbor and Public Works committee.

James, who had noticed the shortage of barrels at apple harvest time, and how prices rose quickly when supplies were short, proposed to create a modern cooperage manufacturing plant and the first one in Trenton that would manufacture hoops. The only other hoop mill east of Toronto at the time was one at Marmora started a year earlier.

The new business was to be called the Trenton Cooperage Mill* and James was the principal owner. He was already contracting for raw material and was planning a first-class sawmill with up-to-date equipment.

James was elected president of the St. George's Society at the end of February. Vice-presidents were B.H. Siddall, W.H. Gill and Thomas Goodsell. The secretary was Thomas Garrett, treasurer A.E. Cuff and chaplain, Rev. Rural Dean Armstrong.

In March, Capt. Alfred Hicks sold his interest in the Steamer *Varuna* to Capt. J.E. Rathbun, who had sailed her the previous summer, and to W.B. Cooper.

James, meanwhile, was away in Ottawa, according to the *Courier*, "on important business in connection with the Cold Storage plant here."

---

*Eben James employed W. A. Fraser in his new enterprise. Fraser wrote to James on December 23, 1905, thanking him for a Christmas bonus and commenting, "I am working for the best man in Canada."

The Trenton market.

A special meeting of town council to consider James' application for riparian rights near his plant and his dredging request was discussed briefly then referred to council's Committee of the Whole.

James E. McCaw, an agent of the Cold Storage dock, was in Toronto, said the *Courier*.

Canadian author J. Castell Hopkins was the speaker at the banquet held by the St. George's Society on St. George's Day, April 23, at the Hotel Gilbert. The *Courier* devoted a full page to a report of the event. Accompanying the article were eight half-tone photographs of society officers including Eben James.

"A delightful evening of speech and song under the banner of Merrie England," was attended by 117 men. "Behind the president's chair was an illuminated painting of St. George…" Guests included E. Guss Porter, K.C., M.P., and Robert Weddell, president of the St. Andrew's Society. It was growing dark when the meal was finished and the toasts began. Dr. Jaques toasted President James, "the worthy president of St. George's Society of Trenton. I know well you will all agree with me that he is a thorough and typical representative Englishman."

The *Courier* editor noted "President James never believes in doing things by halves."

A lavish souvenir program was produced. The menu featured Baron of Beef and Yorkshire Pudding, Turkey and Cranberry Sauce and Spring Lamb with Green Mint, followed by English Plum Pudding and Hard Sauce. Sir John Macdonald's quote "A British subject I was born; A British subject I will die," and Sir Wilfrid Laurier's comment: "The British Empire means freedom, decentralization, and autonomy; it will live, and live forever," were both included in the program.

.. St. George's Society of Trenton ..

♦♦♦

HON. PRESIDENT
C. L. HAWLEY, L.D.S.

PRESIDENT
EBEN JAMES

1ST VICE-PRESIDENT
B. H. SIDDALL

2ND VICE-PRESIDENT
W. H. GILL

3RD VICE-PRESIDENT
THOMAS GOODSELL

CHAPLAIN
REV. RURAL DEAN ARMSTRONG

TREASURER
A. E. CUFF

SECRETARY
THOMAS JARRETT

CHAIRMAN EXECUTIVE COMMITTEE
C. W. LONDON

CHAIRMAN RECEPTION COMMITTEE
W. S. JAQUES, M.D.

CHAIRMAN MUSICAL COMMITTEE
H. F. WHITTIER

....

MUSIC

During the evening Mr. H. M. Bennett and Mr. Rechab Tandy, of Toronto, will render vocal patriotic selections. Prof. Follick, accompanist.

" A British subject I was born;
A British subject I will die."
—SIR JOHN MACDONALD.

St. George's Anniversary

Hotel Gilbert Trenton

April 23rd 1908

" The British Empire means freedom, decentralization, and autonomy; it will live, and live forever.—SIR WILFRID LAURIER.

" SO CUP TO LIP IN FELLOWSHIP THEY GAVE THEM WELCOME HIGH "--KIPLING.

Dinner ❀

Olives   Celery

SOUP

FISH
Salmon Trout, Oyster Sauce

Radishes   Lettuce   Watercress   Cucumbers

ROAST
Baron of Beef and Yorkshire Pudding
Turkey and Cranberry Sauce
Spring Lamb with Green Mint

COLD MEATS
Ham   Corned Tongue

VEGETABLES
Mashed Potatoes   Corn and Green Peas

DESSERT
English Plum Pudding and Hard Sauce
Apple and Pumpkin Pie
Ice Cream   Assorted Cakes
Apples   Oranges   English Walnuts
Stilton Cheese   McLaren Cheese

Tea   Coffee
English Punch

" I DRINK TO THE GENERAL JOY OF THE WHOLE TABLE."--SHAKESPEARE.

Toasts

MR. EBEN JAMES, PRESIDENT

The King
Proposed by the President.
Responded to by the Chaplain, Rev. Dean Armstrong.

St. George's Day
Proposed by the Sen. Hon. President, W. S. Jaques, M.D.
Responded to by the President.

Other Patron Saints
Proposed by the Hon. President, C. L. Hawley, L.D.S.
Responded to by Mr. R. Weddell, President St. Andrew's Society, and Mr. T. A. O'Rourke, LL.B., P.M.

The Empire
Proposed by the Secretary Mr. T. Jarrett.
Responded to by Mr. J. Castell Hopkins, F.S.S.

The Dominion
Proposed by the President.
Responded to by E. Guss Porter, K.C., M.P.
M. B. Morrison, M.P.P.
F. J. Farley, M.D.

....

MR. B. H. SIDDALL, VICE-PRESIDENT

Defenders of the Empire
Proposed by the Vice-President.
Responded to by Major Arnott; Capt. Bywater.

The Town
Proposed by the Vice-President.
Responded to by Mayor Funnell; Coun. P. J. O'Rourke.

Volunteer Toasts

GOD SAVE THE KING

St. George's Society of Trenton Anniversary program April 23, 1908.

CHAPTER 4

The Hastings Rifles

Eben James' development of the shoreline around his dock did not sit well with some people. On May 4, 1908, a Mr. Crouter addressed council claiming that he and other boatmen were being denied access to the shore which had recently been cut off by a boom.

James, present at the meeting, was surprised to hear he was being described as the "offender" and in reply said there was ample room for boatmen to land at the end of the street. "At any rate," he said, "Mr. Crouter would have to deal with him and his company if they wished to use any part of the shore owned by the company."

Water in the bay, lake and river was very high in May, 1908, the highest in 20 years. The high water had caused much damage to property along the shore during winter storms.

James E. MacCaw, described by the *Courier* as an agent of the Cold Storage Dock, was reported to be in Toronto.

Eben James was present at a banquet tendered by about 50 "citizens, friends and admirers" of Molsons Bank manager T.A.G. Gordon who was retiring. The new manager, H.A. Thomson, was transferred to Trenton from Ridgetown.

Following the banquet James left for a month long trip to England. On his return he began to enlarge his fledgling cooperage business.

James distributed a printed flyer in 1908 seeking to purchase apples and offering cooperage stock and made-up barrels. His Toronto address is given as 103 Union Station, his Trenton address, care of T. & A. Storage, and his Montreal address as 224 Board of Trade. He also advertised as having agents at St. John and Portland during the winter season. In addition to Woodall & Co., Boyd Barrow & Co. and N. Isaacs & Sons, he was also representing Bristol Fruit Brokers Ltd., Bristol, England.

In July, 1908, Eben James was gazetted a Lieutenant of "F" Company, 49th Regiment, Hastings Rifles. Lt. James does not appear to have gone to Barriefield Heights Camp, Kingston for summer training that first year.

In August, James received a postcard from a friend in New Westminster, B.C. asking "When is the wedding coming off, or is it all off? Let me know and I will send you a pair of bedroom slippers." The signature is illegible.

Canadian apple exporters had been concerned about the competition in the profitable English market from Tasmania and New Zealand. Canadian trade commissioner P.B. Ball, who was stationed in Birmingham, warned

packers about allowing poor quality shipments being included "like those of last year," or "not much will be heard of Canadian apples in Great Britain."

"This is an unpleasant statement," he continued, "and every care should be taken by Canadian growers to maintain the reputation of their produce in the important old country market."

In September, 1908, in order to help improve the early apple market, the Dominion Government secured cold storage space on steamers sailing from Montreal undertaking to pay for all the space not taken, in this way testing what could be done with early apples on the British market.

James office was still located in Toronto and in October, the *Courier* observed he had been back in town for some days.

A teaser advertising campaign started in the *Courier* in November when reports of a rumored breach of promise case were printed. The case turned out to be a mock trial under the auspices of the Governor Simcoe chapter of the Imperial Order Daughters of the Empire. When the trial was held on Nov. 10, many leading citizens took part with Eben James playing the part of court crier.

Tax collector O.W. Kemp's reminder of taxes due published in the *Courier* was quite blunt. "Pay your taxes and keep clear of the bailiff. This is a final notice."

In January, 1909, town council prepared a bylaw transferring "certain lands" on East Wharf Street to the Trenton Cooperage Mills and an advertisement from the new company sought suppliers of elm, ash, soft maple, stave bolts, basswood, heading bolts and elm hoop logs delivered to the mill yard.

Officers and NCO's of the 49th Regiment (Hastings Rifles).

49th Regiment (Hastings Rifles) Badge.

Lt. Eben James is riding on the gun carriage.

Meanwhile, James returned to town from a trip to Montreal.

On April 8, the Trenton Cooperage Mills began its season's operations although William Fitzpatrick, the mill buyer was taken ill with pneumonia while visiting Millbridge and placed in Belleville hospital.

The *Courier* editor visited the new cooperage mills and found some 80 or 90 men employed, "making it one of the liveliest places in town."

"The installation of an additional large heading saw and two extra motors gives them a capacity of over 200 horse power, and puts them in a position to handle their enormous cut for the season, while the erection of a large well equipped dry kiln and cooper shop, with numerous other improvements makes it possible for them to handle larger quantities of all kinds of barrels and cooperage stock, as well as adding greatly to the appearance of their plant."

The company's intention is to make a specialty of apple barrels, the editor added.

An accident at the mills in May injured A.J. Clark who had been putting a belt on a machine when a stick he was carrying came into contact with a pulley striking him in the chest, breaking his ribs. He had difficulty breathing and his injury was, at first, thought fatal. He did, however, recover from the injury.

A letter, dated May 31, 1909, written on the P & O line ship SS *Moldavia*, from E. Townsend, who recalled travelling with James as a passenger on another P & O ship. He acknowledges James' letter from the previous February, mailed to Calcutta, India. This had been forwarded to Townsend who was spending three months in England. Not much time, Townsend said, "after six years in exile." James, who made frequent voyages to the old country from Canada, was unlikely to consider his life here "exile".

49th REGIMENT (HASTINGS RIFLES.)

7th Infantry Brigade.

3rd Divisional Area.

Organized G. O. 14 Sept., 66).

Regimental Headquarters—Belleville, Ont.

1st Battalion (8 Companies).

Company Headquarters.

A Co.—Belleville.   E Co.—Tyendenaga.
B Co.—Stirling.   F Co.—Trenton.
C Co.—Sidney.   G Co.—Bancroft.
D Co.—Madoc.   H Co.—Marmora.

Honorary Lieut.-Colonel—✄ (**D**) Bowell, Colonel *Hon. Sir Mackenzie, K.C.M.G., ret.,* 19 Mar., 03

Lieut-Colonel.	
D)Ketcheson, W G .... 1 June 12	
Majors (2).	
Ketcheson, W H. .... 1 Jan 12	
Bywater, A E (*m s c*) (E) .... 5 Jan 15	
Captains (8).	
b Green, D (E) ....27 Apr 05	
Ketcheson, F G ....14 June 07	
h Bleecker, C A ....27 Mar 08	
c Vanderwater, R (E)..................30 Dec 09	
g McLean, J L......................30 Apr 10	
e Wilson, H R (*m s c*)......., ...10 June 12	
23 Apr 10	
(*temp maj* 29 June 15)	
Sills, J H (*r m c*) (E) ....11 May 13	
Miller, A P (*rmc*) (E)................. 1 July 14	
f James, E............................14 Jan 15	
b Walt, C F .... 1 July 15	
Lieutenants (16).	
b Danford, S..........................24 June 10	
h Garrison, F McK (E)..............17 Feb 12	
g McConnell, H B.....,..............13 Apr 12	
Solmes, T W..........................1 May 13	
c Graham, W. D................. 2 Jan 14	
a Ketcheson, W H F (E)............... 2 Nov 14	
e Hambly, G H......................16 Dec 14	
d Smith, W L (E)..................17 Apr 14	
f Gwynn-Craig, E G (E)............. 4 Dec 14	
h Bateman, G S (E)................15 Mar 15	
h Dowling, V C......................19 May 15	
a *Wilson, D D...................... 1 Jan 11	
*Foster, L D......................22 Mar 14	
g *Nugent, W L......................13 Apr 14	
d *Watson, C R..................... 1 June 14	
a *Ullyot, A A......................14 June 14	
f *Brandon, E F......................31 Dec 14	
h Gladney, E M.....................19 May 15	
g Wallace, W W (E).............. 2 Dec 14	
d Moffat, T E......................13 Feb 15	
e Powell, S H...................... 1 Mar 15	
b Richardson, B H.....................13 Mar 15	
*Elliott, R J (E)......................20 Apr 15	
f *Fraser, W A...................... 1 May 15	

h Bertrand, M.....................19 May 15	
e Bissonnette, D F.............. 1 Aug 15	
c *MacConnell, E L.................. 1 Aug 15	
a *Williams, V H..................11 Aug 15	
f *Raymond, S J..................17 Aug 15	
e *Sills, R.................. 1 Sept 15	
Adjutant.	
Sills, J H *capt* (*rmc*) (E)............... 2 Mar 08	
(extd 2 Mar 18)	
Instructor of Musketry.	
....	
Signalling Officer.	
*Ketcheson, F G *capt*.................12 June 11	
Quartermaster.	
Nugent, J A *hon capt*................... 4 Jul. 07	
Medical Officer.	
Alger, H H *maj*.....................24 July 05	
(*hon lt-col* 21 July 15)	
Chaplain.	
Blagrave, *Rev R C hon capt*.............15 May 14	
———	
Corps Reserve.	
2nd Battalion.	
Majors (2).	
....	
Captains (8).	
....	
Lieutenants (16).	
Louttit, A M........................ 2 June 10	
30 Nov 05	

Militia List November, 1915. Eben James was a Captain and W. A. Fraser a Lieutenant.

Prescott county. Nearest bank at Plantagenet. Telegraph. Population about 100. John Smith p m

Hughes & Harkin, cheese mnfrs
Lauzon F. hotel
Quesnel Palnia, blacksmith
Smith & Hughes, general store

TRECASTLE

In Wallace township, Perth county 30 miles north of Stratford, the county seat. Moorefield is the nearest railway and banking point. James Christie p m

TRENT BRIDGE

On the Trent river in Seymour township, Northumberland county, 40 miles north east of Cobourg, the county seat and 3 south of Havelock its nearest railway and banking point Stage daily to Campbellford and Havelock. Population about 75. Miss Edna M Pollock p m

Davidson David, saw mill
Dingman I general store
Dingman R M, general store
Vanderburg Charles, blacksmith
Watson Stephen, blacksmith
Wright T & Son, fishing tackle

TRENTON

An incorporated town 101 miles east of Toronto, on the Trent river at its confluence with the Bay of Quinte, and on the G T and C O Rys. which cross at this point, in Hastings county. 12 miles west of Belleville, the county seat. The southern terminus of the Trent Valley canal. The Canadian Northern Toronto-Ottawa passes through Trenton. It was incorporated as a town in 1881, and has saw, flour and paper mills, machine shops, engine and bridge works, canning factory, two large stave factories & cooperage mills and other industries. Presbyterian, Methodist Catholic an Anglican churches, high public and separate schools, an opera house, three banks and two weekly newspapers, the Advocate and the Courier. Assessed value of real and personal property $1,402,148. Bonded debt $153,450.62. Rate of taxation 25 mills. Over eight thousand horse power developed within the limits of the town. The cheapest power in Canada. The town is lighted with electric light and has a good system of water works and a fire brigade. Timber, lumber grain and produce are shipped. Steamboats run daily to Belleville and Picton and daily and weekly to Montreal and other lake ports. Stage daily to Belleville. Telegraph, telephone express. Population about 4,500. James B Christie p m

Abbott Archibald. Barrister Solicitor Etc

Aberdeen Hotel H A Cook prop
Advocate The, P J O'Rourke prop
Anderson John W, butcher
Apple Produce & Cold Storage Warehousing Co, Eben James mngr
Auger George, grocer
Auger George F, boots & shoes
Anger S Miss, grocer
Badlam W E, pianos & organs

_An Ontario Gazetteer and Directory for 1910-11 lists Eben James as manager of the Apple Produce &
Cold Storage Warehousing Co., Trenton._

"I like you have not married, of course," wrote Townsend, "it is foolish to say I never will be, but as long as I have to live in India I hope I shall steer clear of the double state."

James' itinerant lifestyle at this time also made it difficult for him to develop long-term relationships.

Townsend congratulated James on his improved prospects with the new mill.

James purchased an automobile in the summer of 1909. Trenton now boasted eight automobiles and one motor cycle. Another car ordered by Bruce Powers was expected to arrive shortly. Despite the arrival of the automobile, said the *Courier,* carriage-builders in the United States claimed the demand for horse-drawn vehicles was greater than it ever was.

Clem Nugent, who was involved with the Cold Storage for many years, was also a Captain and Quartermaster with the 49th Regiment and in June, 1909 he left for Kingston to prepare for the 12 day camp. Some of the officers were disappointed with the militia department's decision to only send a half-strength unit to the camp and Capt. A.E. Bywater decided against taking any men this year.

Rural Dean (later Canon) F. W. Armstrong.

The apple crop was expected to be heavy in 1909 and the Trenton Cooperage Mills asked farmers to contract early for barrels promising "lowest price, best value."

Later reports predicted the Northumberland and Hastings counties fruit crop would "hardly reach medium" and early varieties were reported as "rather small."

Trenton Cooperage Mill's barrel factory burned to the ground on Tuesday Sept. 23 about 8 p.m. Three men had been working in the mill repairing some machinery when one of them noticed smoke coming from the barrel factory. They sounded the mill whistle and the town hall fire whistle repeated the warning. The glare of the fire attracted a large crowd. Fortunately the direction of the wind prevented the fire from spreading. The loss, partly covered by insurance, was estimated at $3,000.

The company was soon making barrels again and the work of rebuilding began immediately and no major setback was experienced.

A week after the fire the *Courier* said the building had been rebuilt and that the company was awaiting delivery of new machinery and expected to be in full running order within a few days.

St. Andrew's day was celebrated at the Hotel Gilbert in Trenton for the 47th consecutive time and the toast to "The Army and the Navy" was given by Eben James, "whose remarks proved he was at home with the subject."

James name was included among those nominated for council at the end of December although he declined to run. Seventeen persons were nominated for mayor, 24 for council seats and 10 as school trustees. "It was one of the liveliest meetings ever held in Trenton, a spade being called a spade," said the *Courier*. The meeting did not break up until midnight. Dr. Edward Kidd was elected mayor by acclamation, and nine persons ran for the six council seats.

On Wednesday, Jan. 19, 1910, the Governor Simcoe Chapter of the Daughters of the Empire held their annual ball in the Cold Storage building with Bodley's Orchestra of Toronto providing the music. Ladies' tickets were $1 and gentlemen's $2.

A large deputation of citizens attended the council meeting on April 4, to hear Canadian Northern Railway proposals to bring a rail line through town. The line was to cross the Central Ontario Railway line near the cooperage mills and go between the skating rink and the canning factory cutting a small corner off the skating rink and a larger one off the canning factory.

In April, the *Courier* editor visited the cooperage factory to see what had been done since the fire and during the winter shut down. He found the plant had expanded and that the former factories operated by Deer River Mills and W.H. Matthews had been incorporated into the Trenton Cooperage Plant, making the plant "as large as any in Ontario."

The plant's location meant timber could be brought in over the ice during the winter months, by water in the summer, as well as by rail over the C.O.R. "All they want up there now, is a real fancy office to show the plant up, which we hope to see soon."

In April, the *Courier* reported the sale of the Cold Storage building and Wharf to the Trenton Cooperage Mills. The Cold Storage was transferred to the cooperage mill as collatoral for loans. James at this time, owned both businesses.

James addressed council on April 2 and again asked to carry out some dredging near the Cold Storage plant leading down to the Trenton Cooperage Mills.

King Edward VII died and Mayor Kidd declared the day of his funeral, May 20, "a day of public mourning." On that day a procession formed on the Market Square and, headed by the IOOF Band, and followed by the Mayor, Councillors, Board of Education trustees, officials, ministers, fire brigade, school children, fraternal societies and citizens, marched to the Opera House for a memorial service.

Mayor Kidd was in military dress and Rural Dean Armstrong read the burial service, "the same as was being read over the body of Edward the peacemaker at St. George's Chapel, England." Eben James was one of a number of citizens to give a short address. "After singing God Save the King, the procession re-formed and marched back to the Market square."

Another small fire on Saturday, June 18 damaged some cooperage stock near the C.O.R. station, the fire brigade attended promptly and the damage was minimal

Early in July, James left for England to visit the various companies he represented in Canada.

The United Kingdom 1910 apple crop was predicted to be the worst known for many years, providing good prospects for exporting Canadian apples.

CHAPTER 5

Acclaimed to Council

On Thursday evening, August 29, 1910, fire again struck the Trenton Cooperage Mill. The fire brigade had already been called out at about 8.15 p.m. to a house belonging to Thomas Knox, a blacksmith. The roof of the house was burned and the interior of the building damaged by smoke and water.

While the engine was still on the wharf a second alarm was heard and the firemen were told the Trenton Cooperage Mill was in flames. A delay was experienced in getting a team of horses to draw the engine and only a favorable wind spared the town from a more serious fire.

The mill building was destroyed, an active bucket brigade preventing the fire from spreading.

The Cooperage Mills, at this time, employed about 130 persons and most of them found themselves unemployed. The company immediately obtained a heading machine, however, and with the large amount of stock on hand were able to fill orders.

The loss was a serious one and Eben James, speaking at the September meeting of the Board of Trade said his loss was greater than it had needed to be because the fire brigade had taken 40 minutes to get to work on the fire. He said he did not know who to blame for this.

Dr. Jaques explained the firemen were at another fire at Mr. Knox's house when the alarm came in for the fire at the stave mill but E.T. Marsh said he thought someone in control of the fire department was at fault for the delay. J. R. Cunningham said the delay had come about partly because of the lack of heavy harness for the second team of horses and it was recommended that the town purchase two sets of heavy harness, keeping the additional set at the fire hall.

Early in October, Messrs. Morden and Loomis erected a new 40 by 80 foot cooperage mill on five acres of land purchased from the Central Ontario Railway and near the C.O.R. gravel pit. The new company, Loomis-Morden Cooperage Company, had $30,000 capital. The directors were Chester Loomis of Michigan, and H.B. Loomis and W.A. Morden of Trenton. By mid-October the main building was complete and a smoke stack was being erected. It was intended the new cooperage mill would be in operation by the winter.

Meanwhile, with commendable energy, the Trenton Cooperage Company rebuilt their mill and made the new structure as near fireproof as they could.

Robert Weddell

The outside beams and uprights were of steel set in concrete, the building metal-sheeted and roofed with corrugated iron sheets. The boiler house was enclosed in concrete walls and covered with iron beams and roofing. When in full running order, said the *Courier*, the Company provided employment to about 120 workers.

In a little over a year the H.B. Loomis Co., Ltd., sold their entire plant to Trenton Cooperage Mills Ltd. The deal included the Loomis timber limits. The Loomis plant was closed out and the machinery was moved to the Trenton Cooperage property. The price of barrels would not be affected by the sale, said the *Courier*, the price for the season being 38¢ each.

A report on cooperage production in Canada in 1910, compiled by the Dominion Forestry Branch, Ottawa, said 133 firms had responded to their inquiries, 94 of which were in Ontario, manufacturing both slack and tight cooperage. Because the hardwood forests in Canada were greatly depleted, manufacture of "tight" cooperage (usually oak) had dropped while "slack" cooperage (elm and spruce) for carrying such products as flour and apples had increased. Tight barrels were used as containers for oils, alcoholic liquors and other liquids.

In December, the Trenton & Murray Union St. Andrew's Society held their 48th annual dinner and President Robert Weddell was presented with a "Loving cup" and address. The address said Weddell, a contractor and engineer, had been a resident of Trenton for 37 years and that the year, 1910, was his 60th anniversary. One hundred signatures were appended to the address including those of Eben James, Robert Fraser, W.A. Fraser, Dr. W.S. Jaques, A.E. Bywater and J.E. Rathbun. James, President of the St. George's Society and P.J. O'Rourke, President of the St. Patrick's Society replied to the toasts to "Sister Societies."

A strong municipal contest was expected for mayor and council in 1911 but surprisingly, Jesse Funnel was acclaimed as mayor. Edward Kidd had earlier announced his intention of running for office but did not do so. Acclaimed to council were James H. Dickey, Owen E. Fortune, Eben James, E. T. Marsh, P.J. O'Rourke and William J. Preston. The inaugural meeting of council was held on January 9 and James was appointed to the finance, harbor and public works, streets and sidewalks, committees and was named chairman of the printing and bylaws committee.

New companies coming to town usually asked council for a free site and "reasonable fixed assessment." Two companies had made such requests recently including a pearl button factory and an ore concentration plant and ratepayers were to vote on these, in addition to a bylaw to establish a free library.

The Courier reported "Alderman James was a picturesque sight on Friday last, scooting about town in his "Chatham" "monoplane" getting out votes. He worked to good purpose, too, and put into practice the "preaching" of his

Trenton Cooperage Mills.

public utterances on the Bylaw propositions. That's the kind of public men we need more of!"

The three bylaws carried, the pearl button factory by 493 to 23, the concentration plant by 503 to 10, and the free library by 378 to 111.

The Canadian Pearl Button Company Limited was a new company in town. The company president was from Lacrosse, Wisconsin but Trenton investors included W.H. Matthews, W.H. Gill and Capt. A.E. Bywater. The company, which manufactured pearl buttons, began with 24 men and within a few months was employing 35 men.

James was still involved with the Board of Trade and in April he was appointed, with H.A. Thomson and T.D. Bigelow, to a committee charged with preparing a report on the future industrial development of Trenton and to find ways of publicizing the town.

In April, the schooner, *Katie Eccles*, which had wintered at the Cold Storage dock left for North Fairhaven, New York.

In June, Lt. James joined Capt. A.E. Bywater and 50 militiamen, members of the Hastings Rifles, at militia training camp in Kingston.

Trenton was proposed as the Divisional Point on the Toronto-Ottawa branch of the Canadian Northern Railway, a distinction that had also been sought by Belleville, Deseronto and Napanee. The railway required 240 acres to accommodate their yards and buildings which would include a 30-stall roundhouse and a machine shop. The railway wanted the municipality to exempt them from municipal taxes for 10 years and also to contribute $14,000, which would have to be raised through debentures, towards the cost of the roundhouse and machine shop.

The bylaw authorizing the $14,000 bonus to the Canadian Northern Railway carried early in September. The former piling grounds of the Trenton Cooperage Mills to the south of the main railway tracks were to be used as

Snow storm in Trenton, 1912. Left: the Dr. Jack Farley home.

freight yards. Sir Donald Mann, vice-president of the CNR arrived in Trenton in his private rail car to inspect the new rail bridge. He was accompanied by Alex Laird, general manager of the Bank of Commerce. Sir Donald went on to Picton where the party was joined by George Collins, general manager of the Central Ontario Railway.

"The National Land and Fruit Packing Company has leased the Trenton Cold Storage property and will make Trenton its base of shipping operations", said the *Courier* on Sept. 14. "This is the large concern which leased a great number of apple orchards in Prince Edward and Hastings Counties. Its operations are on an extensive scale – perhaps the most extensive of any single apple company now doing business in Ontario. It has paid good prices for orchards and will endeavor to make its profit out of improved methods of orcharding. The Company will hand over a large amount of money to local farmers this fall.

A newspaper announcement invited apple exporters to ship their apples by the R. & O. steamer *Belleville*, leaving the Cold Storage wharf every Wednesday at 7.30 a.m. arriving at Montreal on Thursday afternoon and connecting with ocean steamers leaving for Liverpool, Glasgow and other British ports sailing on Friday and Saturday. The local rate to Montreal was given as 25¢ per barrel, any quantity. "For further information as to export rates call at Cold Storage or phone No. 18."

A friend of James, from Durban, Natal, South Africa, whose name was not revealed on the postcard, wrote in November saying that she had not heard from him for some time. "I trust you are keeping well – making a fortune by the barrel, I suppose."

James decided to spend Christmas in England and Scotland in 1911, the first time he had been home for the yuletide holidays for the past 15 years. As he would be away from Trenton during the nomination period of municipal council he wrote a letter to the *Courier* stating his intention of seeking re-election.

"You have had a hard-working and conscientious Mayor, and most of the Council have spared neither time nor labor to bring in industries, which owing to the general trend of manufacturing and monied interests is always uphill work anywhere but in a large town or city. Thanks to the Council, helped by the Board of Trade and local support, you have new industries that promise a steady and healthy growth and compensation for the loss of the Gilmour Door Co., beside the C.N.R. Divisional Point."

"As a Council we have absolutely no apologies to offer nor excuses to make. The complaint of a few about travelling expenses is unworthy of notice."

James said true public service small or great honestly rendered is its own reward and a duty each owes his fellows.

"I have promised to serve again if wanted and in the event of an election if you want my services you can vote accordingly, if you don't we shall be just as good friends and I shall be relieved from the responsibility."

Capt. A. E. Bywater

Nominations for mayor, councillors and school trustees took place in the Town Hall on Friday, Dec. 22. The Mayor and Councillors gave an account of their stewardship in the past year and Mayor Jesse Funnell and Councillor J.H. Dickey announced themselves as mayoralty candidates for the 1912 term.

The 1912 council was elected by acclamation. Mayor Funnell was re-elected and the new councillors were Owen Fortune, P.J. O'Rourke, E.T. Marsh, Thomas Arthurs, Henry Curry and John Sansom.

Eben James may have changed his mind about seeking re-election. It is more likely that he left instructions to drop his name if his nomination meant the cost of an election rather than an acclamation.

James returned to Trenton in mid-February after his prolonged trip, the *Courier* editor observing he looked well and had enjoyed a pleasant trip.

During James' absence fire had destroyed the historic Opera House in east Trenton, built in 1890, the building being consumed in a fierce blaze, "burning like a bonfire" within 15 minutes. The City Steam Laundry, which was being fitted up on the ground floor, was destroyed as was the adjoining grain elevator. The east end of the covered bridge had also been threatened.

By the fall, R.W. Weller announced he was building a new Opera House on Ridgeway Street. Weller had first considered building his Opera House in Oshawa but, possibly as a result of the opportunity provided by the fire, decided on a Trenton location.

James attended the Board of Trade annual meeting on Feb. 28 where W.H. Matthews succeeded Capt. A.E. Bywater as president. The secretary, Arthur Jones retired as he was moving to Belleville to manage the Molson's Bank there. He was presented with a gold-headed walking cane and a chime clock for his wife.

The Weddell Company dredge Togo.

"Eben James said Mr. Jones was a fine all round man and regretted him leaving here but found solace that we would see Mr. Jones quite often in his motor boat and at duck hunting time he would be on the spot," said the *Courier*.

The first two sections of the Canadian Northern Railway's 30-stall round-house were completed by mid-March. The railway had also constructed a 65 by 100 foot machine shop and a boiler room and had installed a 60,000 gallon, 45 foot high water tank.

In April, many of Trenton's leading citizens took a trip on the Central Ontario Railway to Picton on a gas-electric car, the first of its kind in Canada. Railway officials on the trial run were George Collins, general manager; G.A. Hoag, superintendent; J. D. Evans, civil engineer and George Sprentall, Trenton Station manager.

Among the citizens who took the trip were Rev. F.W. Armstrong, Robert Weddell, W.H. Matthews, O.E. Fortune, E.T. Marsh, P.J. O'Rourke, W.A. Bleecker, J.G. Squier, C.G. Young, W. Pogue, A.M. Harvey, H. McQuoid, T.W. Jacques, B.H. Siddall, E.V. Illsey, S. Hooey and Thomas Flynn. Eben James must have been away, otherwise it is unlikely he would have missed such an occasion.

Eben James, who crossed the Atlantic by liner on 55 occasions during his lifetime, must have been shocked to learn of the sinking of the *Titanic*, on the fifth day of her maiden transatlantic voyage, with the loss of some 1,300 passengers on April 1, 1912.

Harmony and goodwill did not always prevail in Trenton and civic strife was often caused by political differences. An anonymous letter writer had some unpleasant criticisms levelled at Englishmen published in the Trenton *Advocate* and Eben James rebuked him.

The Editor of the Trenton *Courier* said James' response, if anything, was "too mild."

"The only fault we have to find with Mr. James is that of leniency in rebuking the low and cowardly author of the anonymous letter complained of. The greatest coward on earth is the man who stabs in the dark, and, anony-

Eben James I, Founder

Eben James II, President

Eben James III, Chief Executive Officer and Chairman of the Board

Mawnen (Babe) James

Advertising memorabilia from the Eben James I papers.

View of the village of Trent Port from the hill on the west side of the river. 1842.

An aerial view of Trenton

mous letter writers can be counted in this category. They generally get all that is coming to them in the long run."

In May, the steam barge *Iona* of Trenton, bound from Sodus Point to Montreal, laden with soft coal, caught fire off Kingston and sank. The crew were able to take to the boats and landed safely in Henderson Harbour, N.Y. The barge had been built in Trenton in 1892, on the east side of the river bank and launched on July 25 of that year.

Another fire struck the Trenton Cooperage Mills company on Monday, June 17, 1912. The plant had only just started up in the morning on the Loomis Mill property. Linemen were cutting wires when fire broke out in the cooperage shop. The fire spread to a warehouse containing about half a million staves, "which shot up and burned several power poles."

In August the Weddell Company dredge *Togo*, which had been working for some time on a government contract in Thornbury, Ont. returned to Trenton. The barge had been given a civic send-off the town band leading a procession from the town to the waterfront. Hy. Pedwell, who had been the President of the Apple Produce and Cold Storage Warehousing Company in Trenton when it was chartered in 1902, presided over the proceedings.

"With whistles blowing the tug steamed out with the dredge in tow and the long journey to Trenton began. With favorable weather the trip will occupy twelve days," said the Thornbury *Herald-Reflector*.

The Weddell docks on the east side of the river presented a busy and unusual sight on Friday, Aug. 26, 1912, according to the *Courier*.

The tugs *Minitaga* and *Aurelia*, the dredge *Togo*, the drill boat *Quinte*, a steam tug and derrick, the Dredge *Trenton* and numerous other dredges, tugs and scows were docked, "a quarter of a million dollar plant in the harbor, all in a No. 1 condition'" said the editor. The company's full fleet, at this time, consisted of 56 boats, 18 of them under steam with a new drill boat, and the *Meg*, under construction.

CHAPTER 6

More Disastrous Fires

The 1913 municipal elections were looming and Eben James and many others wanted to return Mayor Jesse Funnell to office. Politics played a big part in the elections and Funnell faced considerable opposition.

An announcement, headed "Requisition" signed by 172 citizens, including Eben James and W.A. Fraser, ran in two issues of the *Courier*, calling on Funnell to run for mayor. At the nomination meeting eight candidates were nominated for the office and six declined leaving Funnell challenged by Dr. Edward Kidd.

Twelve persons, including Eben James, were nominated for the six council seats. Dr. Kidd defeated Funnell by 468 votes to 378 votes. Elected as councillors were B.W. Powers, J.H. Dickey, R.A. Lewis, R.H. Spencer, H. Curry and W.H. Waldorf.

Mayor Kidd showed himself a diplomat when he invited the executive of the Board of Trade, which included Eben James, to meet with town council to discuss such projects as the Canadian Creosoting Company proposition. This company, which intended to open a plant for creosoting railway ties, between the Canadian Northern and Canadian Pacific Railway lines, wanted some unopened streets in the area closed and the company's assessment fixed at $10,000 a year for a 10 year period.

Many of the defeated candidates for council, including James, were on the Board of Trade executive committee.

At the Board of Trade annual meeting on Jan. 27, A.E. Cuff was elected president. James urged town council to "break away from the village methods of conducting the town's business," and argued the town could not develop industrially unless it was prepared to spend money.

"He urged that a larger and more progressive policy be adopted by the town authorities," said the *Courier*.

James was appointed chairman of the Board of Trade manufacturers' committee with G.E. Matthews and J.H. Sills as members. The committee was established to look after the interests of the home manufacturers, as well as helping others to establish businesses in town. He was also appointed a member of the banquet committee.

Another fire struck Trenton on Friday, Jan. 24. The blaze started in Sutcliffe & Sons dry goods store and destroyed two business buildings including the J.J. Haines Shoe Store and threatening an entire block. Shurie's Drug Store received smoke damage. A Canadian Northern Railway engine with two flat cars was sent to Belleville to bring back a fire engine to help fight the fire but before it was loaded a telephoned message said the fire was under control and the engine would not be needed. Damage was estimated at $60,000.

On Feb. 7, 1913, Harriet I. E. Thomson, wife of Robert Fraser, died from heart problems. She had moved to Trenton, 30 years earlier as his bride. Fraser had been the local manager of Molson's Bank when it was established in 1880. She was survived by her husband, Robert, one daughter Jeanie (who was later to marry Eben James I) and three sons, William, James and Donald.

In February, council approved the purchase of a new Ronald fire engine, and decided to keep the old engine to provide additional protection should two fires break out simultaneously in different parts of town.

Robert Weddell gave a banquet at the Gilbert House on Feb. 20, for the volunteer fire brigade members, and "representative citizens" and 55 attended.

"Mr. Weddell stated, that as one who remembered the old days of civic strife in Trenton it was a source of congratulation to himself, and he thought to all good citizens, to note the harmony and goodwill prevailing between the civic authorities and the Board of Trade," the *Courier* said.

Eben James made a dynamic speech, full of predictions for Trenton, "which he was assured would be fulfilled. He said that Mr. Weddell "was an active business man, and if we all followed his example in regard to pushing Trenton to the commercial forefront, the result would be that we would soon have a flourishing city here. He hoped the secretary of the Board of Trade was right in saying the knockers were dead."

A branch of the Canadian Club was organized in March and Col. Ponton of Belleville and Mr. Cuff, president of the Board of Trade addressed the meeting. About 100 business and professional men attended and more than 60 joined.

The Trenton Cooperage Mills opened up for another season on April 1, 1913 with 125 employees. The previous year the firm had made 125,000 barrels and 25,000 kegs.

The company had added saw mills to their plants at Trenton and Deer River and acquired more timber limits as well as additional water power.

Just as the plant opened for the season, a gale destroyed the three large smoke stacks at the Company's works. The storm uprooted trees, blew chimneys down, destroyed windows and overturned silos. Plant manager William Fraser, had been visiting Regina and Vancouver on cooperage mill business at the time.

"Eben James made a dynamic speech, full of predictions for Trenton."

Trenton Cooperage Plant manager W. A. Fraser.

Jeanie Fraser

On April 24, James presided over the annual St. George's Day banquet which was held at the I.O.O.F. Hall. He spoke on the group's patron, St. George and the newspapers described the event as "a gala evening." Most of the town's leading citizens at that time were passionate supporters of the British Empire.

On May 15, fire levelled the Miller & Co Canning Factory, destroying all its contents. The fire spread to the adjoining Barr Register Company, which was also destroyed. The town's new fire engine was brought into service and three lines of hose poured a large volume of water into the buildings but it was impossible to stop the fire's progress. Damage was estimated at over $100,000.

It had taken too long to steam up the new fire engine, the *Courier* claimed. The newspaper suggested firemen should be employed to attend to the engine all the time, "the cost of wages being small compared to the losses caused by fire."

Lt. Eben James, of F Company, 49th Regiment, left for the annual encampment at Barriefield Camp on Monday, June 16 where he would command the company in the absence of Capt. A.E. Bywater who had been appointed to the staff of Colonel Sam Hughes, the minister of militia.

Jeanie Fraser* wrote to Eben at camp and spoke of her late mother. "I can quite understand your feeling a bit down for the reason given and it is quite natural," Eben replied. "We only get one mother. I never had any to know and no one can fill her place even (if) it is a sad old world at best and we find so few in our journey through life that are true to us unselfishly."

"Life has never given me the things I have striven for and never will but my lot is only like 90% of the rest so why should I whine, but will keep a stiff upper lip to the end if I can."

James described his early life as "a nightmare...being of an affectionate nature everything hurt. I remember my first day at school, 8½ years old...with never a friend that understood me or to whom I could even really confide and I got in the habit of always keeping my own counsel very young...

James urged Jeanie to "throw her shoulders back," adding, "life will be brighter tomorrow."

The Trenton Cooperage Mills suffered another severe loss in mid-June when 40 per cent of their heading wood was destroyed by fire. The fire bell

---

*W. A. Fraser possibly encouraged his younger brother James, who was working in Buckingham, Que., to write to their sister Jeanie about her relationship with Eben James. The letter dated Sept. 26, 1913, reads: "I discovered a letter of yours written possibly two or three weeks ago and as you are always ready to give good sound advice, allow me to reciprocate in a like manner and discuss freely your apparent serious intentions re: Mr. James. As you have never mentioned Mr. James but in a casual way, I am or might be jumping to conclusions. But tell me, do you ever think of him seriously and if so, when, why, where and how often. Forget it and seek that absorbing work which you so strongly endorse and advise for other people. Perhaps you are a bit sore at Willie's actions and intend getting even with both him and Blanche. Give up the idea of marrying one far too old to be your father. You are not half as old as you feel and it would turn out to be a vast proposition. You could never reform a man of that age; his habits are questionable and he can never amount to anything..."

The Atlantic Cold Storage Company – "The Evolution of Trenton".

alarm rang about 8:45 in the evening. The piles of heading stored on the piling ground were burning. The fire was brought under control then the hose was connected to the Trenton Electric Pumping Station and water continued to be poured onto the embers until the following noon.

On Friday, June 20, a Canadian Northern Railway shifter moving a railcar on the cold storage dock miscalculated the distance and backed the car into the sleeping quarters of the *"Dragon Rouge"*, a dredge belonging to the John E. Russell Company, which was at the dock. The dredge sustained considerable damage. The occupants of the sleeping quarters had just begun to work so the rooms were unoccupied. The *Courier* said the car could be seen hanging over the edge of the dock minus its forward trucks which had dropped off into the water.

Fire was discovered for the second time within a few weeks at the Cooperage Company's piling yards on Friday evening, July 25. The brigade found difficulty in finding a suitable solid place for the big fire engine to operate from but when water was obtained, the fire was quickly brought under control.

Courier readers were told on Aug. 28, 1913 that the Trenton Cooperage Company was going out of business, having been taken over by a new syndicate. The newspaper speculated one of the businessmen in the syndicate was associated with the Redpath Sugar Company of Montreal. The editor said he had also been told the mill was being taken over by Canadian Northern Railway interests.

A week later the *Courier* retracted the story of the sale and said the company was not closing and was still owned by the original members of the firm, Eben James, President and William Alexander Fraser, secretary-treasurer.

The marriage of William A. Fraser to Blanch Agnes Macaulay took place on Aug. 30, 1913.

Fire struck Trenton again on Sunday, Aug. 31 when firemen were called to the skating and hockey rink where they found "a raging furnace from end to end…doomed to destruction."

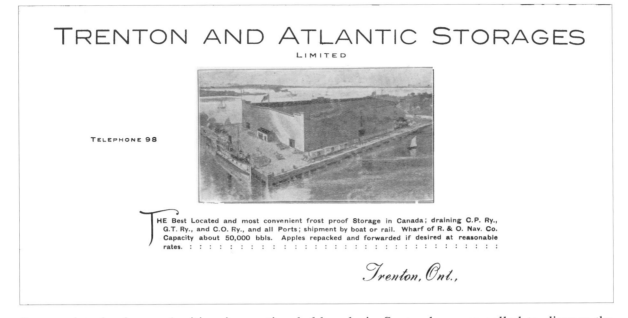

TRENTON AND ATLANTIC STORAGES

LIMITED

TELEPHONE 98

THE Best Located and most convenient frost proof Storage in Canada; draining C.P. Ry., G.T. Ry., and C.O. Ry., and all Ports; shipment by boat or rail. Wharf of R. & O. Nav. Co. Capacity about 50,000 bbls. Apples repacked and forwarded if desired at reasonable rates. :

Trenton, Ont.,

Company letterhead, 1912.

A citizen's meeting held early in September was called to discuss the recent large number of disastrous fires. Ratepayers claimed the present system of fighting fires was inadequate although no blame was attached to the work of the volunteer firemen. The citizens urged the municipality to consider installing a hydrant system.

Rumours of the rink having being used, after hours for "gambling and drinking purposes" and that the fire had been caused by those "engaged in this nefarious work," were denied by Rev. F.W. Armstrong. He said the doors had been locked at all times, that keys were in the hands of reputable people, and that the door's lock had been forced.

In October, a 20-year old man, Earl Henderson, was charged with incendiarism in connection with the skating rink fire, the two cooperage fires, and the canning company fire. The trial was held in Feb. 26, 1914 and the accused was found guilty. Sentence was suspended, the man being bound over to be of good behaviour.

Arson is the hardest of all crimes to prove, said the *Courier* editor, "and where it is conclusively proved, should be given the full limit of the law, regardless of sympathy, age, or any other condition."

C.A. Blohm, an apple buyer for Flavelle's Ltd., in a letter published in the Toronto *Globe*, and reprinted in the *Courier*, urged more government inspection of apples. Blohm said he had purchased 10,000 barrels of apples and had found "the grossest fraud" in the packing and grading.

"Fortunately the fraud was discovered before the apples were shipped out of Ontario, and I now have nearly 7,000 barrels of apples in Trenton in cold storage that had been condemned by the government inspector for fraud in packing.

Eben James, representing the St. George Society, attended the St. Andrew's day anniversary banquet responding to the toast "Canada and the land we live in."

Scenes familiar to Eben James I.

An article by H. A. Thomson (a bank manager and secretary of the Trenton Board of Trade) in a publication entitled *Busy Man's Canada* claimed Trenton, as a place of residence, was "a great improvement of the Trenton of ten years ago. The streets are well lighted, and while not paved, are creditably macadamized."

The Trenton Cooperage Company "does a large business in its line, procuring much of its raw material from the North Hastings limits. This company is also interested in the large storage warehouse, which a year or so ago was modernized at a very considerable expense and is now one of the best fruit depositories in Eastern Ontario. Mr. Eben James is President of this company and Mr. W.A. Fraser is Secretary-Treasurer."

At the start of the year, some five million feet of logs, to be made into barrels, was gathered at the cooperage mill site.

A serious accident took place at the mill in May. Arthur Wallis, an employee, lost his arm in a circular saw accident

In June, the *Caspian* and *North King* steamers began calling at the Cold Storage Wharf rather than the Murray Canal bridge. The town held an Old Boys' Celebration with a giant "Calithumpian parade" and the Trenton contingent of the 49th Hastings Regiment left for military camp at Petawawa under the command of Lts. James and Farley.

Ridgeway Street, Trenton.

The old covered bridge at Trenton was a familiar sight to Eben James I.
Bottom right: Eben's dog "Riley" at the warehouse wharf. The covered bridge is in the background.

CHAPTER 7

For King and Country

C. A. Blohm, who had been an apple buyer for Flavelle's Ltd., leased the Trenton Cold Storage building from Eben James in July, 1914. The wharf, where the *Alexandria* and the *Caspian* docked, continued to be operated by the Cooperage Mills.

"The prospects are for a very large apple crop this year," Blohm said, "and high prices for barrels, and to the small grower this means such prices for apples as the evaporators will pay, for feeding them to the hogs, or leaving them to rot on the ground as they fall."

Blohm, operating as C.A. Blohm Co., Ltd., promised to furnish growers with barrels at market price and gave them the option of picking and packing their own apples or having his company do it for them, the apples to be sent overseas for sale.

Advertisements in the *Courier*, signed by C.A. Blohm Co., Ltd., Lessees, encouraged growers to use the Trenton Cold Storage services for their apples but the beginning of the Great War early in August put an end to Blohm's efforts. No shipping space could be found for barrels of apples.

His final offer to store apples appeared in the *Courier* on Aug. 27.

Blohm later spent six weeks in England and Scotland looking for apple export opportunities. He returned to Trenton saying "the prospect for apple exporting is none to bright on account of the increasing difficulties in transportation."

By Sept. 10, a Trenton Cold Storage advertisement was offering "uncontracted refrigeration or frost proof" space for rent. "There may be many chances to move apples before spring, so don't let them waste." Another advertisement offered buyers barrels "on liberal terms", noting the grower "who has his barrels ready is the one that can sell when opportunity offered…There is every probability that the ocean will be kept open."

An advertisement inserted by Eben James offered to advance buyers $1.50 a barrel for up to 10,000 barrels of standard Fall and Winter apples. "Shippers will receive any balance over freight, commission and advance."

In mid-October, apple growers were being urged by the cooperage mills not to waste their apples, "we will give storage FREE if you can't sell."

A newspaper correspondent from Wooler said the apple situation was "not brightening and prices are rather low."

"While the country man looks on an apple as a necessity, the city man regards these more as a luxury, and in hard times will not purchase."

Loading apples at Rednersville dock.

Meanwhile, war hysteria was spreading. Enemies were being found close at hand. Persons with German names were harried and sometimes interned. In Trenton, Prof. Smidt, owner of many properties in Trenton, protested he was not of German descent but a French citizen. Anyone calling him a German spy, he said, "must cease or the law will be put in motion against them."

The *Courier* told of a dynamite plot to wreck a troop train as it passed through Trenton. The local chapter of the Imperial Order Daughters of the Empire began raising money to buy a hospital ship. The municipality placed an officer on the covered bridge to guard it from fire or other dangers.

The local officers of the 49th Regiment, among them Eben James, were being "twitted" as having "cold feet" by the local ladies because they were not immediately off to war. James speaking at the fireman's dinner explained no rural regiment, as yet, had been called out by the government.

"So far the department has asked for volunteers, not necessarily belonging to any regiment." The 49th was asked to provide 125 volunteers, and had at the time of James' address, gathered 50. "As only three officers are necessary for 125 men, only one was accepted with the 50 and seniority has preference and Major Wallbridge of Madoc received the appointment...the Trenton bunch are ready when wanted."

On Sept. 9, a large assembly of citizens organized a branch of the Canadian Patriotic Soldiers' Fund and Robert Weddell was elected president. Eben James was appointed to the finance committee.

A Patriotic Mass Meeting was held at Weller's Opera House on Oct. 27 and the building was "filled to overflowing." The IODE arranged to give a wristwatch and a package of knitted goods to each Trenton recruit. Officers were to receive binoculars, a prismatic compass and a revolver.

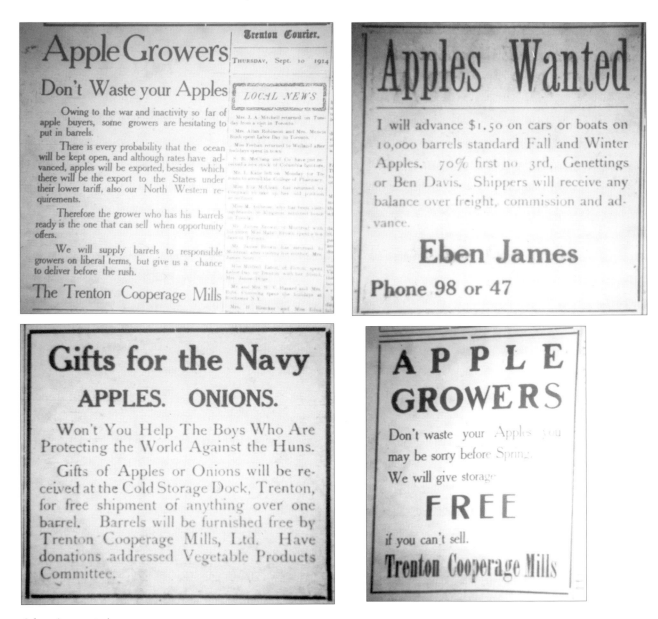

Advertisements in the Trenton Courier inserted by Eben James in July, 1914.

The second contingent left Belleville for training at Camp Kingston on Nov. 3. Among those present to say "goodbye to the boys" were Lt. James, Dr. Jaques, Canon Armstrong and IODE Regent Mrs. G.A. White.

Trenton Cooperage Mills donated $50 to the Patriotic Fund and 64 employees gave sums ranging from $2.25 to 25¢. This list of donors, published in the *Courier*, provides the only remaining list of company employees.

These were as follows: Geo. Henderson, S. Kinlin, B.B. Robertson, E. Bassett. G.A. Perry, Claude Post, H. Hutchison, Neil McPherson, M. Brown, W. Barr, W.S. Dickerson, Thos. Coleman, Geo, Miller, J. Graham, John Carther, B. Hilts, A. Reynolds, A. Craddock, J.L. Post, F. Whitmore, P. Rosse, D. Cushman, Jas. Whirte, Fred Beech. W. Hutchison, A.J. Snare, S. Bassett, Earl Henderson, W. Meteer, D. Sirett, Geo. McGowan, Geo Lesperance, Wm.

Barrels of apples loaded on the barge Waterlily.

Lemp, A. Cooney, John Blight, A. Mountenay, Nelson Cooper, J.E. Hawley, S.Lockridge, J. Parent, C. Wood, A. Paler, H. Brooks, Mr. Philip, J. Hilyer, F. Cooper. D. Noble, E. Ellis, C. Conings, W. Squiers, Peter Storey, L. Bovay, P. Chatupjak, F. Rosse, J. Mikel, P. Campeau, J. Bedard, Jas. Smith, J. Levallie, F. Kittel, J. Woodacre, J. St. John, J. Broe.

Eben James attended the Patriotic Fund's executive meeting on Nov. 10. Canon Armstrong said five Trenton families "were being taken care of which would make a call on the Patriotic Fund of $86.67 per month."

James also attended the 52nd anniversary celebration of the Trenton and Murray St. Andrew's Society, a dinner also attended by Sir Mackenzie Bowell, Col. Ponton and C.J. Bowell. He gave the toast to the ladies "in his usual fearless style, with more or less of Kipling thrown in."

Early in January, 1915, fire destroyed the Central Ontario Railway roundhouse with a heavy loss in equipment. This included the gas electric car, a dining car, the official car *"Bancroft"* and three flat cars. The fire had begun in the paint shop.

Dr. Kidd stepped down as mayor and was presented with an inscribed, gold-headed cane. Acclaimed as mayor was O.E. Fortune.

Canada's minister of militia, Sir Sam Hughes, during a visit to Kingston presented binoculars, a compass and a revolver, to Capt. J. H. Sills of Trenton. Arrangements to deliver the articles on behalf of Mayor Fortune were made by Eben James.

Capt. James, who was now the district recruiting officer, spoke at the annual meeting of the Board of Trade on Jan. 18, 1915.

He said Canadians had nothing to shout about in regard to volunteering for the defence of the Empire, in fact, said the *Courier*, he thought that some drastic measures should be taken to compel men to do their duty in this respect

James also seconded a motion by A. Shurie calling on the municipality to proceed with a Carnegic Library, as decided in a 1912 council resolution.

CHAPTER 8

The Hippodrome

At one o'clock Sunday morning, March 23, 1915, Constable Bain reported the cold storage building on the waterfront to be on fire.

The fire looked insignificant at first but turned out to be a very serious one, said the *Courier*. Black smoke poured out from the windows of the stone, waterfront building and firemen were unable to gain access to the building because of suffocating ammonia fumes.

After a five hour fight, the firemen were successful in confining the flames to the building itself, although it was doomed to destruction. The steam barge *Whitteker*, of the Hall line, a Weddell barge and other vessels were in danger but all were eventually saved with little damage.

During the fire, one of the firemen was carried out of the smoke unconscious, while another fell through the ice, the hose he was carrying preventing him from going underwater.

The loss was estimated at $30,000 on the building and $5,000 on stored apples. The building was under lease to C.A. Blohm at the time.

The 1915 assessment rolls show Trenton Cooperage Mills Ltd., (Eben James) owned the "cold storage plot" as well as the wharf.

James, at that time, was actively engaged at the Trenton Cooperage Mill as well as in recruiting work for the military. This work necessitated many trips, including visits to Montreal.

Town council was considering replacing the picturesque 85-year old wooden bridge that connected east and west Trenton with a new $140,000 steel bridge. In June the traffic on the bridge was surveyed between June 21 and 27 and a total of 47,023 persons had crossed, 5,202 by horse or horse and buggy, 2016 driving automobiles and the remainder on foot. By September the town was offering a contract to the Ontario Bridge Co., for a new bridge and this project was approved by 292 to 42 in a ratepayer's vote.

In August, the steamer *Alexandria*, a familiar sight in Trenton, was wrecked in a storm off Scarborough Heights.

Robert Weddell contributed to the war effort in August, 1915 when he sent a $1,000 cheque to the Department of Militia and Defence in Ottawa, to pay for the purchase of a modern machine gun. He asked that the gun be provided to "our brave boys of the 39th Battalion" and asked if it could be inscribed and named *"Jess"*. The ministry accepted his donation and confirmed they would inscribe the gun as requested.

In August, James advertised for 15,000 barrels of apples and the Trenton Cooperage Mills advertised "the best obtainable barrels," warning growers not to risk profits on their apples by buying inferior products just to save 3¢ a barrel.

In 1915, Council was considering replacing the old wooden bridge.

A patronizing letter from Eben James, published in the *Courier* on Aug. 19, 1915, criticizing the Simcoe Chapter of the Imperial Order Daughters of the Empire as a social organization rather than one deeply involved in war work raised the ire of the Chapter's Regent, Teallie White. This lengthy letter led to further acrimonious exchanges in local newspapers and at recruiting meetings.

"Dear Ladies," James wrote, "is it not about time you reorganized your branch of the D.O.E., and placed it on a war footing and get it operating a bit true to its noble name?" The letter was written because the Regent had refused to allow James, as district recruiting officer, to address a concert audience for a few minutes before the curtain rose.

Appealing directly to the IODE membership, James said the Chapter, appeared to him to be "a one person institution, dominated with an absolutism like unto the Kaiser," and said White's refusal to let him speak was due to the "personal animosity of your chief."

"Hitherto, the D.O.E. has been largely a social organization, and little importance was attached to it," he said disparagingly. "The woman that gives one worthy son, the wife a husband, or the girl a lover, does more for this cause than all the money you collect in a year, though this is essential," he conceded.

James reminded the members that, in the past, on several occasions, he had allowed the use of his cold storage building for their dances.

On Aug. 25, Mrs. White wrote directly to James to object to his comments. She said the letter in the *Courier* was "a malicious defalcation of

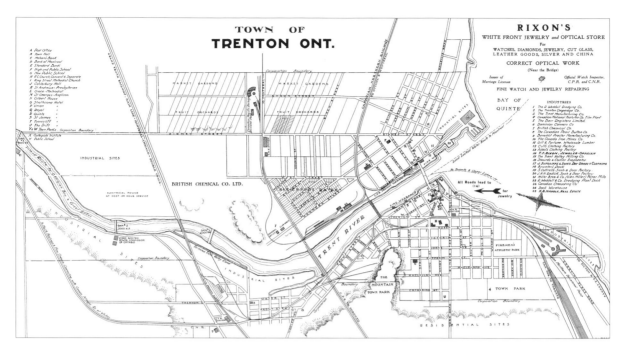

Trenton map given to customers of Rixon's Jewellery (centre, site of British Chemical Co. Ltd.).

myself, both in my official capacity as Regent…and personally." She threatened to take action for his "slanderous imputations" unless he publically apologized. She said she would also write to the Militia Department "to have you disciplined." She said she did not believe the Department would approve of him using his military position "in order to discourage, terrorize and (word illegible) a band of patriotic Canadian women."

Louis George NeVille, the concert organizer, sprung to the defence of the Regent describing James' letter as unprincipled and underhanded.

"Such is my summary of the article in the Trenton *Courier* of Aug. 19th, in which a 'tin' soldier who signs himself Eben James, endeavors to console himself because he was not permitted to openly insult the citizens of Trenton from the stage of the Weller Theatre on the night of Aug. 12th, 1915."

NeVille, who described himself as both a "stranger and also an American," although he was making his living in Canada, said he had always been taught to fight "a FAIR game, and to use the slang, 'be on the level'." Further references such as being "on the square" suggests DeVille was a freemason and he probably knew that James also belonged to that fraternity.

The show, *"Bells,"* he said, was presented as an evening's entertainment, "not as a scheme to get patriotic citizens to the show only to find it was also a recruiting meeting."

This would have been "dastardly," he fumed, adding his time was too valuable to further discuss James' "sneakish and underhand methods."

The *Courier* editor contributed a small paragraph: "It is rumoured that one of our heroes is to be decorated with the Iron Cross by the Kaiser for his gallant attack on some of the ladies of Trenton."

Eben James bounced back with another lengthy letter in reply to the published comments of "that itinerant alien actor."

TORONTO JUL 9 - 1917

CLASS C

License No. 320

TREASURY DEPARTMENT
PROVINCE OF ONTARIO

Moving Picture Theatre License

Issued under Chapter 236, R.S.O., 1914, Amendments passed thereto
and the Regulations passed thereunder.

THIS LICENSE IS GRANTED TO *Ed. James* OF *Trenton* TO EXHIBIT MOVING PICTURES AT *The Trenton Hippodrome* THEATRE *Trenton* AND SHALL REMAIN IN FORCE UNTIL AND INCLUSIVE OF THE THIRTY-FIRST DAY OF MAY, *1918* PROVIDED THAT THE SAID LICENSEE SHALL KEEP AND COMPLY WITH THE PROVINCIAL LAWS AND REGULATIONS AND THE MUNICIPAL LAWS AND REGULATIONS IN THE LOCALITY IN WHICH HE MAY EXHIBIT IN REGARD TO MOVING PICTURE EXHIBITIONS.

Countersigned

Robt. C. Newman
per Q.E. *Inspector.*

Provincial Treasurer.

In June, 1917, Eben James launched The Trenton Hippodrome at the Cold Storage site and obtained a Moving Picture Theatre License.

"Like yourselves I am putting in a lot of time and work for the cause of the Empire without one cent of remuneration and expected I could depend on your assistance, believing the D.O.E. to be something more than a collection agency…"

If a five-minute speech before the curtain rose could spoil a play, he said, then "it is easily spoiled." James said he had been accused of "being ungallant, slandering your Chief, and everything else that is possible and I deny them in toto." His remarks were not malicious, he said, "or anything but a protest."

James said he would be happy to work with the D.O.E. in his capacity as district recruiting officer and he asked the Chapter to invite him to speak on the urgent need for young men to join up.

It appears Teallie White persuaded the IODE National President, Mrs. Albert E. Gooderham, to write a letter of complaint to James' Commanding Officer, Col. Ketcheson. James, in a three-page reply to the National President, said the colonel had already explained to the local Regent that the matter "was quite outside military jurisdiction, and that he was unable to take any action, but believed me to be quite in the right."

James sent one final letter in October to another critic of the IODE affair, H.A. Thompson, who had apparently suggested to some of James' friends that he was unsuited to the job of recruiting officer. Sarcastically, James pointed out that he had "only signed on about 175 men for the infantry (so) I am really beginning to think there is some truth in your statements." It was not necessary to be a member of the militia to do the job, James said, and suggested Thompson might like to take over the position to see how many recruits he could get in the next few months. "Let me know and I will see that you are appointed forthwith."

Future newspaper reports of recruiting meetings involving the IODE do

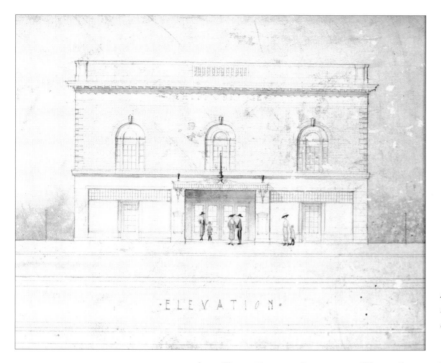

Architects' sketch of proposed Hippodrome at the Cold Storage site.

not mention Capt. James, however. He took part in other patriotic rallies, and at one such rally, held in the Weller Opera House, the *Courier* reported "someone who was after the chairman (Capt. James) tried to create an interruption but was ably answered."

In September, advertisements sought gifts of apples and onions for the Navy. These could be left at the cold storage dock for free shipment of anything over one barrel. The barrels were to be "furnished free by Trenton Cooperage Mills Ltd."

In January, 1916, O.E. Fortune was defeated by W.H. Ireland as mayor, due, said the *Courier*, to "the erratic vicissitude of public opinion."

W.A. Fraser appeared before council on Monday, Feb. 7 on behalf of the Trenton Cooperage Mills calling for better fire protection in town. He said the present protection was for the plant was "entirely inadequate" and he requested a continuation of the water line from the hydrant at Canterbury Hall to Wragge St.

Mayor Ireland called a meeting of citizens on Feb. 15 at the Orderly Room of the 155th Battalion on Front Street to form a local Home Guard unit. The meeting was well attended and some 60 men signified their willingness to join, including W.A. Fraser and his father, Robert.

Fire destroyed the recently remodelled King George Hotel on Tuesday, March 28 and two days later a mass meeting of citizens was called to discuss improved fire protection for the town. Proposed were two more teams of horses, the installation of 12 coal boxes with locks and keys, each to hold about 500 pounds of coal, and a telephone system for alerting firemen.

In May, Fraser was in Chicago on a business trip and James was in northern Ontario buying timber for the cooperage mill. A provincial publication, The *Canadian Courier*, described the Trenton company as carrying out "cooperage on a large scale."

Eben James I

A moving picture company, Canadian National Features Ltd., announced their intention of opening a studio in Trenton. Company president was Jerry Shea of Shea's Hippodrome, Toronto. Construction of their building began immediately and by January a short feature produced by the company was shown at Weller's Opera House.

Within a year the company went into voluntary liquidation pending re-organization.

Mayor Ireland called a meeting of ratepayers on Friday, Nov. 17, 1916, at the town hall, to consider a proposition by the British Chemical Co., Ltd., to erect a plant in Trenton. A wartime project, the preparations were already underway for the company to purchase 134 acres of land. The usual request for exemption of taxes had been made to the town.

By early December, representatives of the Imperial Munitions Board, Ottawa, were in town arranging for the construction of 60 or more buildings on the site. Employment was expected to exceed 2,000. Gun cotton was one of the products manufactured at the chemical plant and some of this was to be stored in the otherwise unused fire-damaged cold storage building.

In February, 1917, James was in Ottawa on military matters and Sir Sam Hughes, the minister of militia, was in Belleville, foreshadowing conscription, noting "The voluntary scheme is slowly fizzling out. Ten recruits could be secured a year ago for the same money it costs to get one at the present time."

James was also active in St. George's Anglican Church where he had been elected rector's warden. James was making plans for the Lord Bishop's visit to unveil a memorial window at the church in July and to consecrate St. George's Cemetery.

In June, 1917, Eben James launched his latest venture – the Trenton Hippodrome. Initially advertised to be in the old cold storage building, the plan was to show, every night, moving pictures and also present "a miniature

Coney Island of Good, Clean Amusement." The general manager was E.S. Stuard, who was succeeded within a few months by A.H. Yeomans.

The Hippodrome did operate for one season although it appears most of the shows were presented on the grounds under canvas. An artist's sketch of the proposed transformation of the cold storage to the Hippodrome survives. This change did not take place, however, but the appearance of the theatre built in later years by W.A. Fraser in downtown Trenton is similar in design. Eben James, had a direct involvement with the Hippodrome and had obtained a provincial projectionist's certificate.

The Hippodrome opened with the movie "His Sweetheart" followed by "Broadway Jones" and "Golden Fetter."

"The Hippodrome opened on Thursday evening with great success," enthused the *Courier*, "if you visited…you were struck with the distinctness and vividness of the picture thrown on the screen." The 12 by 16 foot screen was "absolutely seamless" and "a little lady" playing on a concert grand piano ensured the audience was, "enraptured from start to finish."

The Hippodrome presented many film shows including Charlie Chaplain's *The Pawnshop* and D.W. Griffith's spectacular *The Birth of a Nation*. On at least one occasion, "a sensational boxing bout" was presented.

Anything connected with the war effort interested James, and Mayor Ireland, in July, appointed him to a committee to canvass the town to raise money for the British Naval and Marine Institute.

Two years earlier, an Agriculture Ministry spokesman had warned too many orchards had been set out, "far in excess of the needs of the market and that over-production was certain to result." By September, 1917 it was reported many orchards had been generally neglected, partly because of a shortage of labour, and that "an apple famine" might be experienced in Ontario.

James' involvement in the apple business at this time appeared to be limited to the sale of barrels.

The *Courier* social column noted W.A. Fraser had left for Cleveland, Ohio and that James Fraser, late teller in the Bank of Montreal, Calgary, was visiting with his father, Robert Fraser and sister, Jeanie, on his way to England to join the Imperial Navy. Eben James was in Montreal. The death of former Mayor Dr. W.S. Jaques on Nov. 11, was recorded and Mayor Ireland's brother, Dr. R.A. Ireland was reported killed in action.

An explosion at the British Chemical Company plant on Oct. 14 did considerable damage but within a short time production had been resumed. "The business section of Trenton for the past week has the appearance of recovery from a bombardment," said the *Courier*, "as every other store window has been boarded up temporarily."

CHAPTER 9

Acrimonious Days

On Nov. 8, 1917, a Judicial Notice appeared in the *Courier*, announcing the winding-up of the Trenton Cooperage Mills, Ltd. This action was a consequence of increasing acrimony between Eben James and William Fraser.

Fraser was annoyed because his sister, Jeanie, enjoyed a good relationship with James and this, Fraser feared, would develop into a serious courtship. He opposed the relationship because of a significant age difference between the two. Also, Fraser was a strong Liberal while James was a Conservative Party supporter, and both were active in their political fields.

Fraser – who was a hands-on person – did not hide the fact that he thought he could run the cooperage mills more efficiently than James.

An account from lawyers, Heneker, Chauvin, Baker & Walker of Montreal, dated July 5, 1917, billing for interviews, advice and discussions regarding the cancellation of cooperage mill contracts between James and Fraser, survives in Eben James papers.

The James' papers also include a handwritten agreement, dated March 23, 1910, saying the parties "agreed to work together as one and that the stock held by both could not be sold without either party giving the other thirty days notice in writing." The agreement said the two would "stand together till it is mutually agreed to leave the company…"

Nothing further in the matter of the sale was printed in the newspapers until March 18, 1918, when the *Courier* reported Eben James had purchased all the shares of the cooperage mill, but, "that the future of the business seemed uncertain." In the past, the *Courier* said, the cooperage mill had been Trenton's greatest employer of labour, sometimes using 100 hands in the season.

Some of the company's history is revealed in an undated document (probably written in 1913) headed "Memo. of conversation with Mr. McNally (secretary-treasurer of the St. Lawrence Sugar Refining Company) regarding Trenton Cooperage Mills, Limited: "This business was commenced by Eben James five years ago, who for the previous 12 years had been the heaviest exporter of Apples from Ontario, but finding the price of barrels raised unreasonably any year when demand was brisk, decided in self protection to establish a plant at Trenton, assisted by W.A. Fraser."

"A very capable foreman was brought from the States, who had long experience in operating large cooperage mills, and most up to date equipment was installed, costing $35,974.98, exclusive of five acres of water lot."

Trenton Cooperage Mills and Yards (from "The Evolution of Trenton").

"About this time the apple export trade fell to away below normal, owing to high labor conditions here, poor quality of fruit and large losses of exporters, causing barrel stock to accumulate. The smaller cooperage men threw their stock on the market below cost of production and most of them went out of business; some of the larger ones failed, such as the Canadian Cooperage Company. To add to this a depression was on in the States, and they also unloaded stock in Canada below cost of production."

"Realizing that high class stock was the only kind promising immediate returns the Trenton Cooperage Mills secured the contract of the St. Lawrence Sugar Refining Company at the then best obtainable price, but low figures, for two years.

The Trenton mill had a line of credit with the Bank of Montreal of $35,000. The bank also carried W.H. Matthew's cooperage account. He was the operator of a small mill making only apple barrel heading and staves. Matthews told the bank that he could not compete against the modern mill.

"Then to continue the account the Banker practically insisted that if our credit was to be continued the Trenton Cooperage Mills must absorb his plant, take over his stock on hand, and give him an interest in the business," wrote James.

He took over the Matthews plant and also a half interest in the Deer River Mill, situated four miles from Cordova Mines, north of Marmora, that had been owned by a former farmer and two coopers from Picton. The property provided substantial supplies of timber. A quarter interest of the new operation was owned by W.H. Matthews (assistant manager) and the remainder by G.A. Labey, (timber man), Peter T. Cole (Deer River Mill manager) and W.E. McHenry (a Picton cooper).

In order to manufacture the contracted barrels for the St. Lawrence Sugar Refining Company a credit line of $90,000 was required. This was arranged by Matthews putting up collateral valued at $8,000 to $9,000; McHenry and Labey's collateral was valued at $6,000, and Eben James provided a life insurance policy of $30,000 and the Trenton Cold Storage building as his collateral.

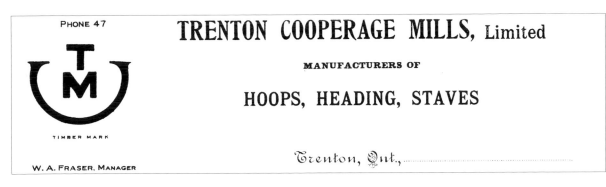

Trenton Cooperage Mills letterhead.

James, in his statement, said too many people were drawing salaries after the amalgamation and costs were too high. "Labey, who was always a farmer till recent years, was unfitted for the timber end...Peter Cole, as Manager of the Deer River Mill was a misfit, being really a Cooper and no practical Mill Manager. W.H. Matthews was a fifth wheel, and always resented (his company) being absorbed."

Only James and Fraser supported renewing the sugar refinery contract when it expired, the others preferring to seek small contracts.

At the annual general meeting, James informed the other shareholders that he preferred to buy them out, retaining only Fraser, as they both agreed some large contracts should be handled. James offered St. Lawrence Sugar Refineries, Limited an opportunity to buy half of the Trenton Cooperage Mills, Limited stock, paying them in preferred and common stock with the Refinery to help to arrange bank credit to replace that previously provided by the retiring shareholders.

The St. Lawrence company had financial control but James had a seven year contract as Managing Director and President.

The Cold Storage building was not included in the sale, but was to be returned to James as he repaid the mortgage that had been taken out on the building.

"The prospects of the Trenton Cooperage Mills could not be better, both for timber and sales," said James. It can manufacture the St. Lawrence supplies for 10 or 15 years with proper management, and with the use of some Birch or other than Elm Staves.

"Its strongest feature is not only its location for raw material but the fact that it is in the largest apple growing belt in Ontario and controls cooper shops in Colborne, Frankford, Foxboro, Trenton, Wellington, Bloomfield, and Picton, which means the most profitable sale of the No. 2 material which is always equal to the cut of No. 1."

The reformed Trenton Cooperage Mills Ltd., was incorporated on March 20, 1918 and the provisional directors were Joseph Max Bullen, Harold Learoyd Steele, Agnes Porter Traill, Wendell Osborne and William Levy, who was elected chairman. Steele was away on war service with the Royal Flying Corps.

The directors were negotiating with Eben James for the purchase of property for the sum of $60,000. On March 27, James acquired the newly-formed company and became president and W.A. Fraser became company secretary-treasurer and a director. The number of directors was reduced from five to three and these were Eben James, W.A. Fraser and H.L. Steele.

Business relations between James and Fraser were at a low ebb by the end of 1920, in fact, James believed Fraser was attempting take over the business. A letter from James to Fraser, dated Dec. 17, 1920, claims Fraser had a "fraudulent scheme to annex my shares for your own benefit." He continued: "I may have been a fool to trust you and your statements but I did and unless I get a satisfactory reply to this letter at once I will hand the whole matter over to Montgomery (James' lawyer) and you can deal with him and not with me as I will leave the whole matter in his hands and ask him to issue a writ against you and the Company and the Bank and investigate the whole transaction."

James outlines in the letter the troubled business relationship between them. He said he had started the Cooperage business as an auxiliary to his apple export business to operate in connection with the storage, "putting up at that time, as my books show, $13,500, you not contributing a dollar. The Export Apple Trade received a serious set back, and I, with other exporters, was almost broken financially, having little else but an equity in the storage, and investment in the mill."

At this time, James said, he had obtained the St. Lawrence sugar contract, which persuaded the bank to extend a line of credit.

"The trouble between you and me started from that date. You threatened to go to Montreal and upset my arrangement, unless, I gave you certain concessions, you were not entitled to. This (on) the day before the money was to be paid. Then you asked for a division of salary, so I gave you $500 a year from mine, making yours $2,000 and equal to mine."

During this time, James said, Fraser never worked loyally with him, and never missed an opportunity to put himself ahead, or to put James at a disadvantage.

James said he had stayed as managing director of the plant after he obtained a militia commission in the 49th Regiment at the start of the First World War because McNally had asked him to do so. Nevertheless, he said, McNally had warned him that Fraser would try to "undermine" him. Despite this, he said, he persuaded McNally to install Fraser as manager so that if his application for a permanent commission was approved, he would be able to leave for military service.

An embargo had been placed on exporting apples during the war and with the increased cost of labour, bank overdraft expenses continued to increase. The St. Lawrence company sent an American employee to the Cooperage to review the plant's operation.

"Whatever your part in this affair was I do not know, but I do know that from your house, where this man visited, the report came (from Fraser's sister Jeanie), that there would be changes in the business, your position (would be) improved, and I should be fired. So that, when the telegram came calling a meeting, I knew exactly what would happen, namely, I was (to be) condemned for bad management."

James, in his review, said he had been "discredited" and made the "goat." The business "was never really insolvent as results prove." James issued a writ against the company and the St. Lawrence company, in turn, "threw the business into liquidation, and claimed they had acted on information received from you in firing me."

The cooperage was put up for sale, by the assignees, and James bought it in his own name, obtaining the money from the bank, Fraser and James agreeing to divide the company equally.

"We found it hard to work together, and the following spring you said the business 'would not keep two,' and you wanted to run it entirely, insisting on making the contracts and doing work usually undertaken by me. To make peace, I consented to this, meantime finding myself out of employment, and (with) $28,500 invested in the cooperage mill, although I had been running it." James said he had also paid a book keeper and a stenographer, "though you were drawing $2,000 per year as secretary to do that work."

James alleged he had asked Fraser the price of barrels required to pack apples and had been told to wait until Monday before buying. Fraser, he claimed, had called a meeting of area coopers and raised the price to $1.50, "causing me a loss of 25¢ to 35¢ at least on several thousand barrels."

James said he had put all the money he could earn outside into the cooperage business to cover the lean years and said Fraser had not contributed any money.

"Now I have reason to believe and I charge that you obtained my interest and shares in the business by a trick, by fraud and fraudulent misrepresentations by which I was induced to part with my shares...I claim that you have not only defrauded me but also the Government by misrepresenting the profits of the business. I had no such knowledge of the operations of the Company as would enable me to form a clear idea of the value of my shares but relied entirely on your statements.

James devotion to Frasers' sister, Jeanie, appears to be the only reason why he did not sue Fraser for misrepresentation and fraud.

Company minutes dated Sept. 9, 1920 record W.A. Fraser, Donald T. Fraser and James O. Fraser as shareholders and that Eben James and L. Steele had ceased to be shareholders and directors. W.A. Fraser was elected president. James had decided to sell out his company shares and resign as president. He and Jeanie Fraser had decided to be married in January, 1921, and they were aware it would be impossible to work amicably with Fraser in the cooperage business.

The company, with Fraser as president, continued successfully for many years but by 1948, the precarious position of Canadian apple growers because of the closing of the export market to Britain had begun to impact on the cooperage mill. The problems continued and production of barrels declined until, in 1957 cooperage buildings were being dismantled rather than spending money on their maintenance.

In 1958, it was decided to wind-up the affairs of the company.

The full circumstances that led to James' decision to sell his share of the cooperage company to Fraser are not known, but it is certain that James was offended over Fraser's actions to the day of his death. Relations may well have deteriorated further after James' marriage to Fraser's sister, Jeanie. James' last will and testament has an oblique reference to the way he was treated by Fraser – without mentioning him by name. The situation was difficult for James because Fraser was his brother-in-law.

For the rest of his life Eben James resented the way Fraser had managed to wrest control of the cooperage business from him. In later years, James strived to find another cooperage business willing to open a branch plant in Trenton or elsewhere in Ontario to challenge Fraser's company.

As early as August, 1922, James was in touch with the Mitchell Cooperage Company of London, Ont. asking them to quote on the supply of apple barrels delivered to Trenton.

James wrote to the Berwick Cooperage Company of Berwick, N.S. on Aug. 19, 1925, noting they sent circulars to Ontario seeking barrel sales, and suggested they expand here. He offered "to handle a shop" in the province for them if they were interested. They declined the offer but said James could represent them as an agent in Ontario.

The relationship between Fraser and James continued to be prickly. A letter from William Fraser on Trenton Cooperage Mills, Ltd. letterhead, dated Oct. 13, 1921, to Eben James who had been inquiring about some of his private property still at the mill testily begins: "Replying to your first question, I do not recognize any claim from you." Specifically what these claims were is not known because James' letter has not survived, but they may have related to a payment for shares James owned. James had asked for payment of $25,000 American for 30,000 company shares and had been told, through the Standard Bank of Canada that they had received $12,315.40 for his account, the Canadian equivalent of $10,000 American. Eben James II thinks it is possible W.A. Fraser never paid the balance due on the shares to James.

Fraser, in his reply, told James that all his papers, books, etc., would be delivered to Mrs. Simpson (James' landlady) "as requested, although I find it is necessary to break the lock off one of the drawers as I do not presume there is a key for it."

He was asked to forward two revolvers belonging to James. Fraser said he was sending the automatic but could not locate "the smaller one."

On Nov. 10, 1920, Fraser billed James for $1,050 "to loss on 3000 barrels not delivered (as) part of cooperage sale agreement."

In May 20, 1924 James wrote a lengthy letter to W.B. Roadhouse, provincial deputy minister of Agriculture telling him barrel prices had risen because the two large producers left in Ontario had entered into a trade agreement which kept prices high. In Nova Scotia, last season, the contract price on barrels was 40¢, reaching 45¢, compared to a 90¢ price in Ontario.

James estimated the cost of a modern cooperage plant would be $45,000, with equipment costing an additional $15,000. Apple growers and dealers

Logs on Trent River being brought to the Trenton Cooperage Mills.

were unable to finance such a plant, James said. He claimed that he could manufacture and sell barrels in Ontario at about 60¢ using the timber limit in Northern Ontario for which he was willing to pay the regular Government stumpage.

He was looking for the ministry to guarantee the bonds on such a company and he offered, by way of a guarantee and security the Trenton Cold Storage property. James had, at this time, also been into preliminary negotiations for the sale of the property to a milk evaporating company.

"I was for many years the heaviest exporter of apples from Ontario and had a cooperage plant which I operated in self protection until three years ago when I sold out and took a holiday," he told the ministry.

The minister in his reply said he felt the proposal was "unworkable from the government standpoint".

James also had discussions with various apple exporters testing the waters for a co-operatively financed cooperage plant in Northern Ontario. Fred Barker of Toronto said he didn't think James would make much headway with the proposal because the business of exporting apples had, for the past three or four years, been very bad, and shippers in Ontario generally had not made any money, in some cases they had lost heavily.

In July, 1924, James was in correspondence with the Algoma Central and Hudson Bay Railway Company regarding the establishment of a stave mill on their line. Nothing appears to have come of this proposal.

He also contacted The Sutherland, Innes Co., Ltd., of Chatham, Ont., inquiring about supplies and stating his intention to start a cooperage company "in a small way".

CHAPTER 10

"Worried about Business"

The terms of the Great War Armistice were accepted by Germany and hostilities ceased at 11 a.m. on Nov. 11, 1918. The war was over.

The residents of Trenton went wild over the news, steam whistles sounded, bells rang, and displays of patriotic bunting appeared in every window. The Mayor declared a holiday and veterans held a parade amid general scenes of rejoicing.

The British Chemical Company, still engaged in repairing the damage caused by the munitions explosion, was ordered by the Imperial Munitions Board, Ottawa to discontinue work on the T.N.T. and gun cotton lines. The smokeless powder plant was to continue to operate for a time.

The end of the war also brought to an end negotiations Eben James had entered into to lease the fire-damaged Cold Storage building to the chemical company for $150 a month, plus $25 a month towards the taxes, with rent due from the time the building was ready for occupation. He had requested one year's advance payment to assist in the cost of roofing the building. The chemical company had, for some time, been using a part of the building to store gun cotton.

An influenza epidemic that was sweeping across the world reached Ontario and on Oct. 15, the Trenton Board of Health ordered all schools, theatres, and churches closed and banned public assemblies of any kind. Influenza again swept the world in 1919, and in Trenton, as elsewhere, many people succumbed. On June 2, 1919, James prudently prepared a will in case he became an influenza victim. Across Canada, some 50,000 people died, almost as many as the number of Canadians killed in the First World War.

James, in this will, proposed to leave his English cousin, Ashley Tindall Clarke of Loughborough, $10,000 free of tax, Helena Laura Clarke, Frank Clarke and Winnifred Clarke, each $5,000 free of tax.

St. George's Church, Trenton, was to receive $750 for a memorial window to be inscribed: "To the Glory of God and in memory of a wanderer who worshipped in this Church for ten years." The window was not to bear his name.

His personal effects, at his Trenton lodging, (Mrs. James Simpson's, Victoria Ave.), were left to Mr. and Mrs. Chas. W. Smith of Toronto. Specifically mentioned were his Grandfather's clock, clothes, books and a coon coat. Mr. Smith was asked to visit Trenton and to destroy all his private letters.

Lizzie Tompkins of the Portland Hotel, Victoria, B.C. (a former girlfriend?) was to receive "a lady's ring in my tin box" and $2,000.

Four houses he owned in Northampton, England were left to Ashley Clarke.

The balance of his estate, estimated at between $10,000 and $13,000 was left to Miss Jeanie Fraser of Henry St., Trenton. This will, as well as James' final will, both contain an indication of a quarrel, the one he had with Fraser. "But (I) desire my executors to go into the affairs of the Cooperage Mills Ltd., very carefully as to stock and all holdings to establish valuation and secure same to avoid annoyance to Miss Fraser or argument over same with W.A. Fraser."

Should she decline this bequest, the money was to go to St. George's Church, Trenton.

The executors were again warned that "The Cooperage should be handled carefully to get value for same. The trouble will be to get a purchaser to act with W.A. Fraser who will no doubt try to get (the) whole property at a low valuation. Advertising in *Barrel & Box & Coopers Journal* might bring results, I being president and hold controlling vote."

Even in his last will dated July 26, 1948, James referred to his problems with Fraser, although he did not mention him by name: "I further enjoin the family to try and pull together as a unit. I pay my tribute and thanks to God who in spite of the rottenest opposition the Storage Company has been enabled to carry on..."

The Cooperage Mills matter had ended with the sale of the plant to Fraser. The Cold Storage plant was in limbo and James decided to take two years off and spend it in England. Before leaving, however, James had made one more decision. He proposed to Jeanie Fraser, and the two were married on Jan. 14,

Jeanie Fraser with her father, Robert Fraser, and a friend.

1921 at Saint Luke's Church, Winnipeg, Manitoba. James was 48 years old and his new wife was 32 years old. The couple spent the winter in California before leaving for England.

In England, the James family spent time with relatives and friends in London and then rented a house at Mawnan, Falmouth, Cornwall. Their first child, Joan was born on Oct. 15.

Eben James made frequent visits back to Ontario during his stay abroad and was, at this time, becoming involved in the mining business in Northern Ontario. He spent a lot of time at Kirkland Lake, Haileybury, and elsewhere in Northern Ontario and Quebec. For a time, James represented Canada Mines Syndicate Limited, of London, England, seeking opportunities for their investors.

James was also the president of Northrand Syndicate Limited of Kirkland Lake, a company staking land claims in the gold producing areas of Porcupine and Kirkland Lake. Directors were John A. Murphy, Fred J. Browne, A. H. Browne and L. Murphy. He was also associated with the Gowganda Opportunity Syndicate of Haileybury, Ont.

His stay in northern Ontario was lengthy and he and his wife, who continued to live in England and Scotland, kept in touch with daily letters. "You seem to have been away for ages and you don't know how homesick I get for you," Jeanie wrote on July 16, 1922 from Dunoon, Scotland. She observes food was expensive in Scotland, "6d a small loaf of bread, meat 2/4d a pound, vegetables and fruit are terrible...I don't think we paid more for things during the war...it seems horribly extravagant to pay such prices."

"It is so nice to get a letter on Saturday as it is useless to look for one on Sunday and it seems a long wait until Monday," Jeanie wrote on July 23. In this letter she mentions having made inquiries about the cost of passage back to Canada. "The C.P.R. *Metagama* sails on Aug. 11, but I don't know her next trip, she seems to be making odd trips - £32 for a berth but it is far too much. I don't want to waste too much on the passage."

On Aug. 9, Jeanie responded to a letter from Eben expressing some business worries: "I don't mind being 'worried about business' as you put it at all but want to share your life in every way and have felt not doing anything and spending a lot of money is being hardly fair. I do want you to do something that you are really interested in."

In 1924, the Cold Storage Building was being little used and James sought to either sell the property or to find other uses for the building. In February, hearing the National Drug and Chemical Company of Canada Ltd., was looking for an Eastern Ontario location he offered to sell them his building.

The company, however, decided to locate in Kingston.

In August, he offered the building to Mead Johnson & Company of Evansville, Indiana, U.S.A. who were planning to locate in Eastern Ontario. A company representative looked at the plant but decided that it would cost too much to remodel to suit their particular needs. The company decided to erect a plant on a new site in Belleville.

James also came up with the idea of turning his building into a brewery. He felt confident that his political connections were sufficient to enable this to be done.

A letter from James to architect Julius C. Schultz, of Buffalo, N.Y. dated Aug. 22, 1924, refers to a conversation that had taken place between them about obtaining a brewery licence. James said his lawyer, J.D. Montgomery, "assures me there will be no trouble in obtaining same." James asked Schultz if he felt the size of the existing building was sufficient for such a venture. On Sept. 18, James wrote to the provincial attorney-general seeking a licence to erect and operate a brewery at his existing building in Trenton.

James proposed to form a joint stock company with $250,000 capital to be known as the Trent Brewery Limited to manufacture such beer and other beverages for home consumption as would comply with Ontario law, and also to manufacture for export.

James wrote to Schultz to say he was waiting until "a vote is taken for or against Government control on the 23 October next," and "should this fail, I shall pull every wire possible to get the licence in any case, but I am advised to wait in the meantime."

On Sept. 22, the attorney-general replied to his letter, declining to consent to a licence. "As the Government are anxious not to do anything that would add to the difficulties of enforcing the Ontario Temperance Act, I am not

Mineral Dye Products Ltd. letterhead.

prepared to accept the responsibility of issuing the consent requested in your letter. The position I now take is consistent with that which has been taken since we accepted office."

The matter rested until February, 1925 when James again wrote to Schultz about developing a brewing plant.

Schultz noted James' "encouraging news" that the government may be permitting the brewing of a stronger beer in the province of Ontario. The architect said he felt the Trenton buildings were suitable for a brewing plant and that the project was feasible.

James wrote to Gooderham & Worts of Toronto asking if they could recommend a practical brewer. In their reply, F.W. Barron said he knew of a graduate brewer from Great Britain who was on his way to Canada and was "looking for an opportunity to demonstrate Old Country brewing in Canada."

At Schultz request, J. Raymond Schwartz of Buffalo, who sold new and used brewing, bottling and refrigeration equipment, wrote to James offering to look out for a possible partner for his proposed new brewery. Schwartz said he was also attempting to find suitable used equipment.

The government wasn't co-operative and a licence seemed unlikely and James reluctantly abandoned his idea of establishing a brewery.

Recalling his relatives in England were in the dye business, James considered establishing a company to manufacture "mineral paints" or dyes. He had, in fact, already obtained a charter for such a company in May, 1920. Still needing a use for his building, James decided to establish a dye works, to be known as Mineral Dye Products, Limited, "manufacturers of fast mineral dyes."

His English relatives must have had some involvement in the projected project as a letter from lawyers Heneker, Chauvin, Walker & Stewart of Montreal dated Nov. 20, 1919, referred to a Power of Attorney in James' favour, that had been signed by Mrs. Laura Clarke. This authorized him to transfer the Trenton property to the Mineral Dye Products Limited.

The plant and contents, other than the freight shed and dock, was then leased by Canadian Dyers Limited in 1921 and operated under the name of Mineral Dye Products Ltd.

On Feb. 2, 1922, Eben James, writing from Rosewarren Cottage, Mawnan, Falmouth, England, asked the British Dyestuffs Corporation, Ltd., Manchester, if they were interested in taking over a dye manufacturing plant in Trenton, Ont. He said the plant had, in the past year, been leased to a Canadian "who had successfully manufactured dyes for an American firm during the war," and another man, the grandson of a rich banker in Baltimore, who had furnished the capital.

The plant was "nicely under way," James wrote, when the banker died and the estate decided they wished to have the business sold.

"I am not a practical dye man, and have other interests which cause me to spend much time during the year in England, I am therefore anxious to connect with a progressive British concern."

James said a small part of the plant was still being used by the British Chemical Company to manufacture sulphuric and other acids.

On April 6, 1922, Canadian Dyes, Ltd., company president C.R. Wright wrote to James at Mawnan, stating the Company "is in a very critical position."

"While $600 will take care of all accounts which are pressing us, the companies to whom this amount is owned are very strenuous in their demands and are threatening suit. The reorganization of the Company has not been carried out and you must realize that it will be a serious matter for any of these companies to sue us at the present time."

A day earlier, Wright had sent James a telegram stating (B.H.) Siddall (who had been managing the company) was "away indefinitely." The letter that followed the telegram said Siddall had "unfortunately left for parts unknown about a week ago."

Wright said he was of the opinion that "in the interests of Canadian Dyes and of yourself the sooner you get back to Trenton, the better."

On May 19, James wrote to British Dyestuffs Corporation to say he was sailing to Canada the next day on the S.S. *Canada* and would call on their representative in Montreal, Mr. Buxton, to provide details of the Trenton plant.

"I will be interested in Canadian Mining for some time to come, and, as already explained, (I) only purchased the Canadian Dyes Ltd., to keep it a going concern in my premises, and on the advice of my banker, and therefore trust you will find it to your advantage to operate this plant."

James said his address for the next three months would be the National Club, Bay Street, Toronto.

The British company did not purchase the business.

How James solved the problems at the plant is not known but in January, 1925 the company's remaining equipment was sold to the Dye and Chemical Company of Canada, Limited, Kingston, Ont.

The attempt to establish a brewery had failed and the dye business had turned out to be unprofitable. James was still very much involved in mining claims but was also considering returning to the business he knew best – exporting apples to the United Kingdom. James had, in 1921, unsuccessfully tried to represent James Adam, Son & Co. of Liverpool in both Ontario and British Columbia. He did, for a time, do some business with this company, He was, however, successful in coming to an agreement with T.J. Poupart, Ltd., the largest fruit commission salesmen in Britain. This was to lead to a long, and profitable, association.

CHAPTER 11

"World's Finest Produce"

T. J. Poupart, Ltd., of London, Liverpool and Southampton, claimed the "World's Finest Produce" was consigned to them and Eben James did his part by shipping barrels of Ontario's finest apples to this company from the early twenties to the beginning of the Second World War.

The Poupart company at Covent Garden continues in business to this day.

"T.J.P.", as the company was commonly known, was established in 1895 in a small way by John Poupart, who had originally operated a stand at Covent Garden Market where he sold the produce from his father's market garden at Twickenham. The business grew and Poupart began to sell produce for a number of small growers. The "T" of T.J. Poupart was quite mythical. At the time Poupart began his business there was another J. Poupart at Covent Garden so the "T" was added for business reasons.

Shortly after the company was established, William Ravenhill was hired as salesman and became Poupart's partner in 1900. The partners began to confine themselves to the transaction of commission agents' business. The company was formed into a limited liability company in 1905, with Poupart and Ravenhill as directors. Poupart's did not grow any of the fruit they sold nor did they make any purchases.

In the early days the partners did everything themselves. They sold the goods and delivered them, and did their own clerical work, even to licking the stamps. When the company changed to commission sales, it grew rapidly. *The Market Grower and Salesman* for Wednesday, Oct. 31, 1923, quoted Ravenhill as saying the huge block of buildings the company occupied in Long Acre might be called "Poupartown" from its size. In addition to shops and stands in the most central position of Covent Garden, Poupart's had twelve warehouses covering 16½ acres.

Poupart's imported fruit from every part of the world and, after selling it for the best price they could obtain, paid the growers or agents for each consignment, less a fee for the services they provided. Over 3,000 copies of the company's weekly market report were distributed providing a review of market sales and a record of prices realized at Poupart's Covent Garden, Spitalfields, and Liverpool branches. The company employed over 400 people. The general manager was W.H. Press, a former Director of Marketing at the Board of Agriculture.

James had first exported apples from Ontario to England in 1896 to Veitch,

Eben James letterhead.

Moir & Erskine of Edinburgh. By the 1920s he was the largest Ontario exporter of apples, the majority being shipped to Poupart. James, through Poupart, advanced money to growers for their shipments and barrel purchases and pre-paid freight charges. James had met Poupart's William Ravenhill in London in 1921 and proposed a business relationship but nothing developed until August, 1925 when James again approached the company by letter suggesting shipping boxes of apples, packed as a "jumble pack," rather than in barrels.

Ravenhill welcomed James' approaches but said apples packed in boxes as "jumbles" would not cover expenses and said barrel shipments were better, even though they cost more. He offered to advance $1 plus freight for each barrel of good sound export stock. This amounted to a $2.50 advance and the apples could be shipped to London, Liverpool and Hull, and also to an agent in Glasgow. Ravenhill, in a cable, said he was interested in Spies, Baldwins, Greenings, Russets and McIntosh.

In September, 1925, a Thornbury, Ont. grower, who had done some business with Poupart in earlier years, wrote offering to ship apples through a fruit growers' association. Ravenhill declined his offer noting Eben James of Trenton, "a man I have known in England" was to represent Poupart in Ontario, advancing $1.50 per barrel on his shipments.

James had hoped to persuade Poupart to advance $2 a barrel but agreed to the lower advance. Poupart limited James to shipping a maximum of 500 barrels per steamer as a precautionary measure to ensure they were not "snowed under with several thousands of barrels on one steamer at any one port at one particular period." He also allowed James to add Ganos and Starks varieties to his shipments, although he noted Starks sometimes travelled unsatisfactorily.

James wrote to Poupart on Oct. 13 notifying them 650 barrels had been sent to Glasgow by the Donaldson Line. Noting the market was improving he bemoaned the fact that he had not started buying apples early enough, and "I am trying to be everywhere at once."

Poupart agreed to accept some Ben Davis shipments but again refused James' request to increase the advance from $1.50 to $2.00 "One dollar, fifty is quite enough, even for exceptional packs."

In October, James told Ravenhill he was going to Toronto to speak with the Minister of Agriculture over the fact that just two agents were getting all the government contracts despite promises to the contrary. "I fear there is a

Facing for small, medium and large apples.

nigger in the fence somewhere in the shape of commission refunded to some-body on the inside."

In December, James shipped 1315 barrels, three cars going to Hull, three to London, two to Liverpool and one to Glasgow. Frost had spoiled about one third of the Ontario crop, he estimated. Commenting further on his visit to Queen's Park attempting to get some government business, James repeated his claim that he believed "the under officials have been greased."

James also asked if Poupart was interested in shipments of potatoes but they said they were not involved in the potato trade. Ravenhill said German merchants had also offered to sell potatoes in the United Kingdom, "so apparently that country has a very heavy crop."

His first year of shipments to Poupart was satisfactory to both parties and James said he felt the foundation had been laid for "big business" the next season.

He did not ship exclusively to Poupart, however, continuing for some time to supply some apples to fruit brokers Thomas Allan & Co., Ltd., of Glasgow and Veitch, Moir & Erskine of Edinburgh. In a letter to the Edinburgh company written on July 17, 1925, James reminds them he first shipped them apples in 1896 "and I know what you want."

James actively promoted Poupart in Canada and built up a large business with them. Surviving correspondence shows letters and telegrams passed between James and the Poupart company almost on a daily basis.

The fruit season of 1925-26 was a bad one in the United Kingdom, partly due to the Arsenic-in-Apples scare, said a booklet issued by The Fruit Trades' Federations' "Eat More Fruit" advertising campaign. Arsenic contamination, due to orchard sprays, had been found in American apples. A Royal Commission on preservatives in food reported that more than a hundredth of a grain of arsenic was injurious, yet American apples had arrived in the United Kingdom in which as much as one-twentieth of a grain had been found. American growers had been spraying with arsenate of lead to combat the codlin moth pest.

The fruit trade was also hard hit by a General Strike in Britain in May, as during the strike no fruit could be unloaded or distributed. This, of course, affected James. The booklet described 1926 as a "disastrous year."

T.J. Clogg, the son of J.R. Clogg of Montreal who had employed James in his early years in Canada, wrote from the St. Catharines Cold Storage and Forwarding Company Ltd., saying he had heard Eben James was "back in the game of apples again."

He had no apples to offer but asked James if he was interested in moving any pears, plums and grapes, though not peaches, which were scarce. The young Clogg had got in touch with James through Fraser in April, 1923 after losing touch with him for some time. He said he had recently visited Montreal to retrieve some books he had stored there and had looked up former colleagues to find "the old Fruit game has been killed or (has) broken most of them." His father, he said, had died six years earlier.

James was shipping barrels of apples from Trenton, despite limited demand from the United Kingdom, as an advice from Rob. G. Weddell, Contractor, of Trenton dated Nov. 17, 1925, confirms; 122 barrels of Spies, 31 barrels of Ben Davis, two barrels of Seek and one barrel of Wealthy apples were loaded at the CPR freight shed in refrigerator cars.

A few barrels of McIntosh apples shipped at the end of November were, according to Poupart, "what we know on this side as tickers," or apples too loosely packed. In mid-December some other barrels were landed in "a pilfered and slack condition" and Poupart claimed compensation from the steamship company.

A letter to James from R. Veitch of Veitch, Moir & Erskine of Edinburgh, dated May 3, 1926, also refers to a "disastrous season" and said losses by shippers and dealers "must have been very grave indeed." He saw little opportunity to sell imported apples and ended with a fervent wish for "better times and seasons."

A number of Trenton area growers were unhappy because the sale of the apples did not raise enough money to cover commissions and shipping costs. James, in his reply to Veitch said some apple men had not received back half of the cost of their fruit and are, "in many cases absolutely broke."

In 1927, apples were in short supply in Ontario and James opened an office in Albion, N.Y. and began exporting apples from the United States, both from New York State and Virginia. In a letter to U.K. buyers James said he had noticed that "in view of the shortage of apples in Canada, the Canadian Government recently removed the excess duty, replacing (the) old duty of 90¢ per barrel and 30¢ per bushel." The Albion district, he said, was the only district he knew of where there remained a good quality of hard apple left, the principal varieties being Baldwins and some Greenings.

James wrote to a number of New York growers seeking their business. He told A.E. Curtis & Son, Sterling, N.Y. that he was already shipping for the Wooster Fruit Farms, Inc., Union Hill, Monroe County, and boasted once Poupart got a man's business, "they generally keep it." James, also sought additional business in Ontario and writing to Ben Coyle of Colborne he said Poupart's "seldom lose a shipper unless he dies and that is absolutely correct."

Not every grower was satisfied with the results, however. W.H. Gibson of

Newcastle, who had shipped Russets and St. Balfour apples to Poupart's wrote to James to say he was "certainly much disappointed with the result and it would appear to be folly to export apples from Ontario to England." He said he had found the market there to be so unreliable "that it would be best left to our competitors."

In March, 1927 Ravenhill said he could not explain why the apple trade had been so unsatisfactory of late. The main reason, he thought, was that some shipments had arrived in poor condition "and from your experience you are aware that any fruit arriving out of condition has the effect of more or less spoiling the market for the time being."

Ravenhill said some auctioneers had also knocked some shipments down without any consideration of the shipper "or even of the value of the goods, and by their actions they have undoubtedly helped to depress the apple market generally."

Earlier in the year Clem Nugent had been travelling through New York state seeking apples for James and on Jan. 17, 1927 he wrote to say he had located 50,000 barrels of apples for sale in Gustown.

Market Grower and Salesman advertisement.

Meanwhile on April 21, 1927, James, in a letter to Ross Gates of Ontario, N.Y., was expressing regret that his apple shipments had hit a slump in the market and the sale price did not bring sufficient to cover the advance and freight charges.

James, wrote from Albion, N.Y. to Nugent in Trenton to say both British and American apple sales were "off" and that holders of apples "have nowhere to go." His stay in Albion must have been profitable, however, as he told Nugent he had purchased a new car and was driving home "to spend a few days with the kids as I almost forget what they look like."

Returns from Poupart varied widely and James, in a letter to the company dated May 21, observed "This apple game is the most uncertain thing on earth."

Part of the cold storage building, gutted earlier by fire, was still open to the sky and Canadian International Films Ltd. had used this part of the building to film Paris street scenes and First World War trench scenes for *"Carry on Sergeant."* Tons of sand was trucked in to build the trenches. Overhead piping provided rain.

In 1928, Eben James asked the company to remove the sand from the building and place it on a nearby road. The company agreed and also paid $150 in full settlement of all claims and expenses, in connection with their use of the building.

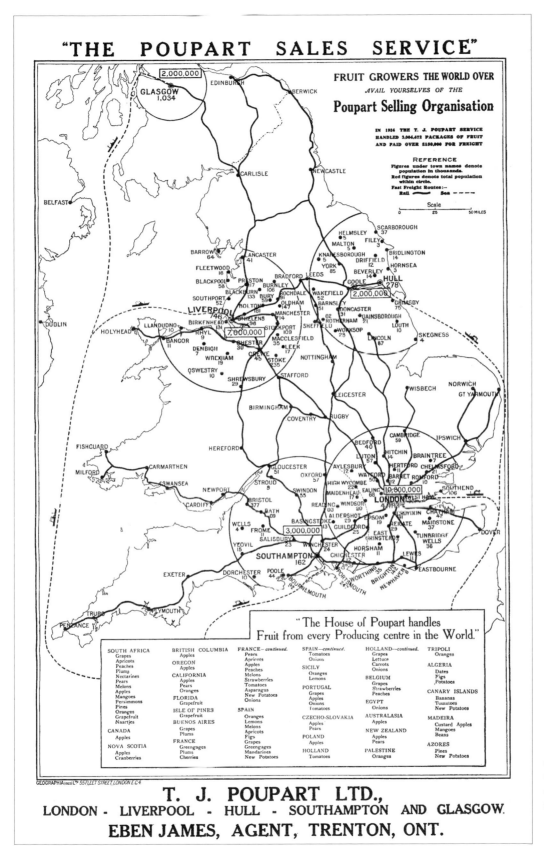

Poupart flyer lists Eben James as agent.

CHAPTER 12

Changes at Pouparts

On Oct. 31, 1930 William Ravenhill died at his home in Claygate, Surrey. He was 56 years old. He had been in failing health for some months having been seriously injured in a motor accident in Cornwall the previous fall. A few weeks earlier, Ravenhill's son, Donald had told James that "the Governor" was progressing well, "and the last time I saw him he was making arrangements with regard to his returning to the Office in the near future."

Poupart described Ravenhill as "a marvellous salesman" who "would stick at business until ten or eleven at night and for a long period made the despatch of our account sales his entire responsibility."

"In general affairs," Poupert told *The Market Grower & Salesman & Fruit Trader*, "he was a man of the soundest judgment, and I myself was frequently glad to go to him for advice."

John Poupart wrote to James on the day of Ravenhill's death saying his partner had died after many months of serious illness. "He always had such a high regard for you, and I feel that I ought to let you know of our loss at once."

Ravenhill's son, Donald, who was involved in the business "and undoubtedly possessing...all the energy and commonsense of his father," took over his father's work. James, however, did not find the younger Ravenhill quite as easy to work with.

Ravenhill wrote to James on Nov. 28 about a shipment of apples from Sharping and Morton and warned him that Poupart's did "not want to advance recklessly." Speaking of U.S. apples, Ravenhill said he did not want to pay "fancy prices to the Yankees, and I shall bleed him for the last ha'penny. In the past I feel that he has had the best of the bargain, and he does not consider our position in the slightest."

"In the case of other countries I always consider the shipper, and I am out to do the utmost I can in his interests, but in the case of the Yankee I am out to get as much as possible out, and as long as I have made a profit I do not care 'two hoots' about the shipper on the other side. They care nothing for us, and all they think of is getting money out of us. In the past they have succeeded, but I can assure you that they are going to find it a tough proposition to get much out of us in the future."

Ravenhill said he trusted that his letter had given James a clear picture of what he thought about the American apple business.

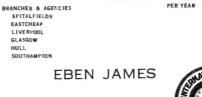

*Eben James'
business card.*

James understood from these comments that Ravenhill was dealing with other shippers in New York State and he was annoyed.

"You talk about passing the order on, which apparently means you are doing business in New York state outside of myself and I think it only would have been fair to me to state that you were making other arrangements. It appears to me that some influence is undermining me with you and in justice to myself, I think you should give me a few facts and a chance to make any explanation, because I have always played the game with you absolutely straight."

In Ravenhill's reply he said his father was always opposed to the direct purchase of fruit and preferred consignment lots. He said Mr. Poupart had agreed to give purchase of American apples a trial during the upcoming season dealing only with brokers.

"Please do not think that I want to do business through other people, and cut you out entirely. My point is, that with the present strong competition in this country amongst the Salesmen, it is absolutely essential that we are able to sell every type of fruit at competitive prices."

W.H. Press also found problems in working with the new management and left the company on Dec. 1, 1930 and opened up under his own name as a fruit, flower and vegetable salesman at Spitalfields Market, with offices in the London Fruit Exchange Buildings.

Press wrote to James on Dec. 22, 1930 to say he had resigned as Poupart's general manager, "the reason being that some days before our mutual friend passed away, I had occasion to speak to Mr. Poupart about an Agreement I held, and about which we differed, but as I did not see any prospect of Mr. Poupart seeing my point of view, I tendered my resignation."

He said he was not soliciting consignments from James, which might conflict with the standing of his late firm, but asked if he would "put in a good word for me with any of your friends."

James replied to Press on January 6, 1931 and, "in absolute confidence" confided that his own dealings with "our mutual friend's son have been anything but satisfactory." James said Ravenhill appeared to be trying to reorganize the whole business and was, at the same time, "making mistakes."

He said he was unable to do business with Press unless, at some time, he made a break "with our old friends" but said he would recommend him to a shipper in Lockport.

James shipped some Greenings to Poupart on the *Aquitania* early in February incurring the wrath of Ravenhill who cabled: "Why go against my instructions? *Aquitania* has no refrigeration. Shall hold you responsible for scald." A letter that followed said he was sorry he had "to wire you in this strain, but under the circumstances I felt that I had to put things rather strongly."

R. and O. Liner at Cold Storage Docks. Trenton, Ont.

Richelieu and Ontario Navigation Company vessel at Cold Storage docks.

A letter from James reminded Ravenhill that he had not included Greenings, but only Baldwins, in his request for refrigeration shipments only. The weather was cold and the shipment should land cool."

"It is all very well for you to imagine that these Greenings are going to land here in a fit condition," Ravenhill replied, agreeing he had not specifically mentioned Greenings but noting brokers representing firms in North America normally asked if cold storage or ordinary storage was required before shipping.

The apples shipped on the *Aquitania* "turned out fairly satisfactorily," with only slight scald Ravenhill confirmed on Feb. 19.

Another unsatisfactory shipment was defended by James as having been checked by Canadian inspectors.

"I presume the gentleman who inspected this particular car was fired for being drunk? At any rate he deserved it," retorted Ravenhill. He declined an offer of some Baldwins as ample supplies of Winesaps remained in the United Kingdom. "I prefer to be contented with the deals which we have had this season, and have now to clear our stocks on hand in preparation for the New Zealand and Tasmanian crop."

Ravenhill said although trade had not been particularly good in 1931, he hoped James had "at least made something out of the various transactions which we have had with you." He reiterated the company's decision to buy American apples in future and cut out commission business except where shipments could be obtained with a very nominal advance.

James said the buyer's market Poupart had experienced in 1930 may not continue and he urged Ravenhill to allow him to continue to quote on shipping apples to them from New York and Ontario, "and possibly Virginia."

The Ontario government was providing him a grant to rebuild his cold storage plant in Trenton, James wrote, "which should give me a fair grip on exports from Ontario."

CHAPTER 13

Distillery Plan Goes Awry

For some years before James made the decision to rebuild the Cold Storage he had been attempting to find a use for his building. His unsuccessful attempt to obtain a brewery licence was followed by protracted negotiations, carried on for over five years, to convert the building into a distillery.

As early as June, 1925, his lawyers McMaster, Montgomery, Fleury & Co. sent a telegram stating "Hear Ontario Government refusing licences." James was confident, however, that he would be able to get a licence if he could interest investors in a distillery.

On August, 1925, James wrote to W.H. Matthews (formerly of Trenton) in St. Andrews, Maryland to say "that American bunch" had leased the Cold Storage for a distillery, "have machinery installed and are waiting for a licence." He also invited Matthews to invest in a cooperage project he was planning.

On May 17, 1926, James was warning the Canadian National Railway agent not to place any cars on the Cold Storage siding for shipment from there because he had not received payment due from the Canadian Distillery Ltd., "and am taking this measure to protect myself for rent," He said he was away a great part of his time and wanted to ensure no machinery was removed from the factory without his knowledge.

James wrote to General Bernard Hepburn on May 17, confirming a recent conversation with him in Belleville about the attempt by Canadian Distillery Ltd., to get a licence. "They made no progress, as you could be sure and are pretty well discouraged for any further attempt." He said he had been approached by another company, interested in buying the property, which intended re-applying for the lapsed licence of the Hamilton Distillery.

On the same day he wrote to G.S. Walters of Philadelphia regarding the lapsed licence and said he had been informed by "the most reliable sources, that they will not be able to do (this)."

James asked if Walters knew of anyone interested in investing in a distillery, stating the cost of a licence would be "at least $35,000".

Two days later, James wrote to J. & D. McCallum, Ltd., blenders and exporters of Scottish whisky, of London, England, asking if they would be interested in being involved in a new Canadian distillery. He said he had been told he could get a licence, "through certain channels."

His property, he said, was ideal for a distillery, with a solid stone building

Dundas Street Bridge, Trenton, Ont.

*Dundas Street
Bridge, Trenton.*

available, deep water dockage, good railway connections and cheap coal supplies. James gave the names of fruit brokers Jas. Adam & Co., Liverpool, and T.J. Poupart of London, as references.

In reply, a company director said McCallum's were aware Ontario had gone "wet" and said they were, at present, concerning themselves with placing their "Perfection" brand whisky on the Ontario Liquor Commission price list. The writer said his company "could not entertain the proposal you put before us."

By the end of 1927 James thought he would soon have a licence and a lengthy letter from E. W. Stanley, mailed from the Hotel de La Salle, Montreal, apparently a resident of England, refers to this: "I was very pleased that you have received the Licence, at least, it looks (so) by (the) Government having accepted money that you will have it."

Stanley was involved with a shipping line and was willing to work with James to bring Cassia (a coarse kind of cinnamon bark used in distilling) to Canada as well as shipping bananas to the United Kingdom.

By February, 1928, James had come to an agreement with Canadian Scottish Distilleries Ltd. of Toronto to turn the cold storage building into a distillery, subject to a licence being obtained. He told the company he had approached town council for an exchange of land, had discussed with them an extension of Albert Street, and also had come to "a gentlemen's agreement" regarding a fixed assessment for municipal taxes.

Councillors had asked how many jobs would likely be created and James said he had estimated 100 persons would be employed.

James set forward his proposal for the property to the municipality in a letter dated Feb. 10. He said The Canadian Scottish Distilleries, Ltd., was capitalized at $4,000,000. "Arrangements have been made with the Dominion Government for the Distillers' Licence, and financial arrangements have been made." The company, he said, intended to purchase the Cold Storage Plant but also wanted to purchase a neighboring three acre lot from the town and they were willing to pay $300 for this and also convey a small triangular section of land to the town.

"The Company proposes installing five stills supervised by a skilled distiller who is being sent out from Scotland, and, in addition, of course, there will be considerable storage and warehouse facilities necessary to carry on the business."

On April 21, 1928, Gordon R. Sheppard, President of Scotch and English Products Ltd., of Toronto and Canadian Manager of the proposed distillery syndicate, told James he had just spent "two strenuous weeks" in Toronto trying to raise sufficient capital to get the Trenton project underway.

"The difficulty has been to find one group financially strong enough to handle the whole thing."

Sheppard said he had been in discussions with a group headed by H.P. Werner, "a very wealthy man and a man who made most of his money at the distilling business in the United States." Sheppard said Werner felt a lot of money could be made from the project and that the distilling business in Canada had a very bright future. However, he estimated it would take at least three or four years "to put this proposition on its feet."

James was unhappy with the delay and on April 26 sent Sheppard "two formal documents" for him to sign, one noting the syndicate's option on the cold storage building had expired and one saying James withdrew his subscription under the terms of the syndicate.

His covering letter expressed the hope that he would still be able to come to a satisfactory agreement, "but in fairness to myself I must say that I can not wait indefinitely and in the meantime I must hold myself free to enter in to any other arrangement with any other person if the same is forthcoming, unless I am assured definitely of a deal with your proposed Syndicate."

Sheppard replied to James' letter the next day observing "a proposition of this kind takes a great deal of time and also a great deal of patience." He said he had "lost no time since January 5th the date on which we received the letter from the Department advising us positively that a licence would be issued."

"I think you will agree with me that a Distillery business with ultimate success in view requires a great deal of capital and in order to get that capital there is considerable checking up to be done by the people who subscribe the money."

"Many difficulties have been encountered, but ultimate success is assured", he said.

It is unwise to become "panicky at this time just as we are on the eve of success."

Sheppard said some investors had questioned the need to pay out $30,000 to $40,000 to acquire a permit which should only cost $250.

"These people fail to realize, however, that the $250 is only a nominal fee and that it requires a great deal of political pull and influence to obtain such a licence at any price."

Another problem in interesting investors in the Buffalo and New York areas, he said, was that another distillery had been started by Col. John A. Currie at Port Dover, "and for which he obtained considerable money in Buffalo." Another distillery in Kitchener had been financed with Buffalo and New York capital.

James' reply was conciliatory. He said he had no intention of letting Sheppard's efforts over the past months "go for nothing," and said the formal notices of cancellation of his option and of withdrawal from the Syndicate were to protect his interests. "I want you to understand that I am still open to make arrangements with you whereby the property, Charter, etc. can be turned over to any Syndicate you may form, but in view of all the circumstances I feel that in the event of any business going on between us new arrangements will have to be made."

Sheppard replied on April 29, promising to have "a good substantial deposit" available within a few days. "In this case it will be necessary to tie the property up indefinitely. The deposit however will warrant that."

In May, James made an arrangements to meet Nelson T. Barrett of Buffalo, an attorney and counsellor-at-law, in Niagara Falls, Ont., later in the week to discuss an offer Barrett had made for his building. This had been for $25,000 cash and a further $25,000 as a mortgage.

"In the meantime you might explain to your parties that I have an absolute guarantee of a licence, also a Charter in the name of the Canadian Scottish Distilleries, Limited, for five hundred thousand dollars, and additional land under agreement with the Town of Trenton and the Canadian Scottish Distilleries, Limited."

"The Government have used me extremely well and have refused to dispose of this licence without insisting that my property goes with it, and if it could be arranged it would suit me better to dispose of everything I hold connected with the proposed Distillery."

James also wrote to Sheppard on May 1 informing him that he had "other parties" after the property who were offering $25,000 cash and a $25,000 mortgage and wanted to close immediately. "Have held them off till Thursday to give you a chance to meet similar terms. I cannot afford to lose (this) opportunity.

This letter crossed with one, also dated May 1, sent by Barrett repeating the offer his clients had made and confirming their claim to already holding a licence. Barrett asked James to be sure to keep the appointment at Niagara Falls, as one of the parties was coming over 500 miles to meet him.

The meeting did not, however, take place as Barrett wrote to James on May 21 saying he had heard nothing from his clients since they made the appointment to meet James in Niagara Falls, "It is reported that they are in Chicago. I do not think it is worth while depending on them seriously."

James wrote to a mining investor friend, H.M. Bishop, to say the Toronto distillery promoters were now asking for another extension and wanted to see if they could raise some money in Canada. He suggested his friend get in touch with Sheppard if he would like to earn some commissions by finding investors.

In July, James was consulting Trenton lawyer Herbert J. Smith asking what he should do about protecting his interests should the distillery proposal falter and the sale of the cold storage not go through. Smith recommended ways James could benefit whether or not the sale of the property took place.

Sheppard managed to find some investors and by the end of the year he was reporting to James on his search for somebody to manage the distillery plant. He came up with Hugh M. Schwab, of Louisville, Kentucky, who had

Bay Quinte, Trenton, Ont.

The Bay of Quinte, Trenton.

spent his life in the distillery business, manufacturing whiskey in Tennessee and Kentucky. Schwab had agreed to purchase $50,000 worth of Class A stock and move to Trenton and personally supervise the installation of distillery equipment and the construction of any additional building which may be required.

A draft of a letter, to be sent to possible investors, dated Jan. 29, 1929, outlined the proposals for financing the distillery. James said the new distillery had a Dominion charter and a guarantee in writing from the excise department that a licence would be granted on the erection of stills and building changes.

He said an old established "Scotch" firm would be providing aged malt and spirit to manufacture whiskey which would bear the label of a well-known brand of Louisville, Kentucky whiskey that had been popular before prohibition.

"The whole proposition is clean, legal, and will bear the closest scrutiny...The directors, of which I am one, are men of integrity that can furnish ample references. One is an ex-member of parliament, who has arranged the licence."

James inserted an advertisement in the New York Times seeking investors and received a number of replies from individuals and from agencies specializing in arranging financing for companies.

Some meetings took place in New Jersey and New York but nothing came of them. "I must admit I am at a loss to know why this proposition does not appeal to your group," James wrote to one potential investor, "...this plant cannot help but make money."

By April, James was determined to bring matters to a head. He wrote to Sheppard telling him that he must show some action at once, "or all agreements I have made will be cancelled."

Sheppard's reply has not survived, but it must have satisfied James because in June he was showing plans for the new distillery to local builders, specifying that the building addition must be of stone and also writing to the C.N. railway to obtain quotes for the delivery of stone, "intended for a distillery building," to Trenton.

The directors of Canadian Scottish Distilleries Limited held a meeting in Toronto on July 21, 1929. Present were G. R. Sheppard, president; John Callahan, director; and B.J. McCormick, secretary-treasurer. The directors agreed to appoint Hugh M. Shwab (sic) as general-manager at an annual salary of $5,000.

In September, James received a letter from National Revenue Canada (Customs and Excise Divisions) from A.C. McFee who said he had noticed in the Daily *Ontario* that, there was, in the near future, a likelihood of the construction of the Distillery at Trenton being proceeded with. He offered

C.N.R. Station, Trenton, Ont.

Canadian Northern Railway Station, Trenton.

any assistance he could give including meeting with James in either Belleville or Trenton.

Early in 1930, James began to hear rumblings that suggested the government was not going to issue any more permits for new distilleries. Writing to Fred. J. Brown, secretary-treasurer of North Rand Syndicate Limited, (Eben James was the president of this mining syndicate) at Kirkland Lake, Ont. he expressed his concerns about the licence. Brown sympathized with him, commenting, "it is a hell of a position to be in but what can we expect except this from such a lot as we have at Ottawa at the present time…"

"The apple business going soft at the same time that the other went wrong must have tried your nerves considerably and I suppose from the way the amendment carried in the Commons that even if the present crowd were turned out that the other side would not repeal it."

James wrote to a New Jersey investor on April 22 in an attempt to find someone willing to put up sufficient money to install the necessary stills and qualify for the promised licence. James said he had been told "on the very best authority" that no more distillery licences were to be granted "and as Canada will be wet for years to come, I am satisfied that a distillery licence in this country is a valuable asset."

Although he had been promised a licence politically, and this had been confirmed by Canadian Customs and Excise officials, James was afraid that an election would be called in the summer or the fall, "and it is advisable that this licence is secured and the matter cleared up before this election takes place, as every indication points to this Government going out of power, but when a licence is once granted, it would never be revoked unless for some serious breach of the Customs Act."

In August, James interested another Toronto investor, A.E. Rae in taking an interest in the proposed distillery but here it was proposed a suitable new building should be erected on a site immediately adjacent to the Cold Storage plant. James was to receive 800 paid up Class "A" shares, 800 fully paid "B" shares and $10,000 in cash for about six acres of land. He also wrote to the Canadian Scottish Distilleries Ltd., advising them that he had withdrawn their option on his building as the time allowed had expired.

A letter from Rae, dated Sept. 4, 1931 stated his principals, "after looking over towns from Prescott to Windsor, have decided that Trenton is the logical place for our Distillery."

In fact, James had known for some time that a distillery was now quite unlikely and had since early in 1931 been making plans to renovate his building and re-open it as a cold storage plant.

CHAPTER 14

Trenton Cold Storage Rebuilt

James had succeeded in negotiating a loan from the federal Department of Agriculture towards the rebuilding of the cold storage plant. Originally, the ministry had promised a grant but, following some political interference by William Fraser, who was now Northumberland M.P., the agreement was changed to a $50,000 loan rather than the promised subsidy. A further $50,000 loan was obtained through the provincial Ministry of Agriculture. The former property, then known as the Atlantic Cold Storage, was purchased by James' new company from his old company by issuing 7,500 fully paid up shares.

W.E. Tummon, M.P., South Hastings, told James he was optimistic the federal payment would be approved by the minister. "I was in conversation with the Deputy and he advised me that your application looked favourable, and gave as his reason the fact that the Minister was feeling that way. Of course, I had already been to the Minister and was there again yesterday."

Tummon advised James to keep "absolutely still about the matter at Trenton and let it come as a surprise and a bit of news when we get it through. I have no worry about Fraser."

At Queen's Park, James had enlisted the help of W.H. Ireland, M.P.P. He provided him with a list of subscribers – Chas. Weaver had 50 shares while 28 other local farmers held 10 shares each – and provided details of the plant's construction and capacity.

According to the Trenton *Courier-Advocate* for April 2, 1931, W. A. Fraser, Victor Little and H. Crews had been meeting with farmers and discussing building a co-operatively owned cold storage building, availing themselves of provincial and federal grants. A suggested location was opposite or near the Borden Malted Milk plant. The capacity of the proposed plant was to be from 30,000 to 50,000 barrels. The estimated cost of construction was $100,000, leaving farmers to raise $40,000 after grants.

Fraser was one of the largest apple growers in Eastern Ontario. He packed more than 9,000 barrels of apples yearly at his 365-acre Glenburnie Farm, 110 acres of which being devoted to orchards. He had purchased the farm in 1911 and had a building capable of storing 3,500 barrels. In October, 1931 he constructed another building with a storage capacity of 5,000 barrels. The farm was managed by Pat Gallagher.

This farmers' cold storage co-operative was never proceeded with, however, probably because it was learned James' plans for re-building were well underway.

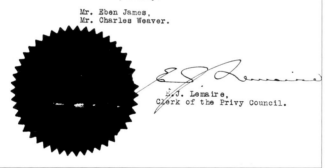

Eben James was appointed to the Trenton Harbour Commission, December 1930.

In fact, a provincial charter had been issued to James on Feb. 25, 1931 incorporating the new company as Trenton Cold Storage Ltd.

It was an opportune time to build the new storage plant. Labour was readily available and wages were low because of the Depression. The provincial and federal governments were offering substantial grants or loans to encourage the construction of cold storage plants and fruit growers, who were exporting their apples overseas, needed cold storage facilities.

Early in June, James told the Linde Refrigeration Company of Montreal, who were providing the refrigeration equipment, that he had been successful in obtaining a grant from the provincial government and expected to receive a similar grant from the federal government shortly.

Appointed foreman for the reconstruction was Hubert Strong of Trenton, a general contractor and builder, who began work on June 15. He was to be paid $87,140 for his work. By mid-July steel footings were in place. The doors were enlarged and preparations made to lay cork insulation and pour concrete on the first floor.

"The work will be rushed right along so that the Cold Storage will be ready for the patronage of the businessman and the farmers during the latter part of the summer. The old fire engine was brought into use on Monday to force the water around the piers and to carry out the earth. This job took nine hours to complete." said the *Courier-Advocate*.

Early in July, a Col. H. J. Smith, a lawyer representing Eben James, met with town council and asked if they would approve an exchange of land with James. The town was offered a triangular section of approximately two acres in exchange for two acres along the waterfront. Smith said the land was required to erect a distillery. The land owned by James had also provided a location for the town's softball diamond.

Thirty-four thousand cases of cork for insulation were delivered on the *Marie Lydia*, a vessel that stopped off at the cold storage dock weekly to load canned goods.

In the first week of August, cork insulation from the Armstrong Cork &

Insulation Company, Ltd., of Toronto, was being laid on the second floor. Twenty-four columns had been installed to support the floor. By mid-August 80 men were working night and day in three shifts to get the building completed and the machinery installed before the apple season.

The *Courier-Advocate* for Sept. 17 predicted the plant would be completely finished within three weeks and farmers would be able to bring in perishable goods for storage. When the main building was completed a shed was to be constructed on the western end of the property.

The building was finished and ready for the packing of apples by early in October, ammonia was turned on into the storage chambers and the freezing process began on Oct. 14, 1931. Already a large number of barrels of apples had arrived and additional large consignments were on their way.

A number of farmers were at the plant when the freezing plant was put into service. G.A. Mackay, Canadian representative of the Wayland Machinery Company of Coresville, Virginia provided a demonstration of apple grading.

Farmers watched the process with great interest, said the *Courier-Advocate*. "Apples were first deposited on a dump belt and from there carried to the eliminator where all trash such as leaves and apples of an inferior quality are taken out. Thence the apples are taken to the polishers and up on the rollers to be sorted for quality – the rollers keeping the apples revolving to show all the defects – the domestic apples going down one side in four different sizes and No. 1 apples going down the other side, also in four different sizes."

In the evening, William Bell, a large apple buyer from Montreal demonstrated the packing of apples in bushel boxes.

Town Council met in special session in September and approved the land swap with James who also agreed to pay the town $300. This was to be a very

C. W. Lott
Mayor

Town of Trenton
Mayor's Office

Mr. Eben James.
Trenton, Ont.

The bearer, Mr. C. Salisbury would like to make application for a position with you in connection with the Cold Storage.

This man has a good education, is very good at figures and a good penman, he can do any class of work that would wish to put him at. He is a good Tory and an Anglican and I want you to see that my friends are taken care of if at all possible.

At the present time he is only working part time at the Paper Mill and he finds it pretty hard going, he has had experience with farming and produce.

April 25, 1931.

MAYOR.

Mayor C.W. Lott seeks a job for "a good Tory".

Town of Trenton
Mayor's Office

controversial deal, however, with considerable public opposition to the transfer of the property. The six members of the town's Parks Board resigned in protest.

The commissioners submitted their resignations "as a public protest" to town clerk P.J. O'Rourke stating they were opposed to the deal as made. They said they had not been consulted about the matter. The chairman of the board of management was D.R. Purdy and members were H.F. Whittier, D.L Jones, J.M. Hennessey, T.H. Jarrett and Chas. M. Richardson.

James wrote to the *Courier-Advocate* on Oct. 21, explaining the background to the land exchange. The wedge-shaped piece of land had been purchased some 25 years earlier and not being required for cold storage purposes at that time he had allowed the Trenton ball team to use the property as a playground, "freely granted for the munificent sum of one dollar a year, to enable the owner to keep title to the property." Meantime, he said, the council had been filling in toward the bay, "but without the storage property, it would have been impossible to use the ground for playing ball."

The taxes paid on the property, without any revenue, were approximately $500, James said, "therefore, unquestionably the storage owners, have contributed more to the Ball Park than anyone else – and contributed something that cost real money, which the public has never known." The property could have been fenced at any time, he added.

The additional $300 James had paid in the exchange had been offered by Council to the Parks Board to enable them to fill more land, he said, and fill was available from the recent sewer line excavations.

James also said the exchange benefitted the town because it enabled improvements at the cold storage plant, which provided employment opportunities. Additionally, "a distillery, using a large quantity of cull apples, which is still being contemplated by the promoters, and who have options on the ground," would provide even more development.

"No sane Council could refuse to exchange it," he claimed. "The wisdom of the exchange is shown by the fact that 100 to 125 men have been employed all Summer and had it been necessary to dispose of the whole Park, it would have been a good bargain. Over one hundred families have had full dinner pails, little children have not been hungry and their parents have a bit to help them brave the coming winter, to say nothing of the work the Storage is furnishing to keep it running, the re-packing of fruit, now and for years to come. Also the fact that it is safe to say this plant is one of the finest ever built of its size anywhere."

"We all like a game of ball and other amusements, but people must eat. If the Storage never turned a wheel, the assistance it has given to unemployment has warranted the exchange of land a thousand times and has saved the town thousands of dollars in relief." The Ball Park is not ruined, he insisted and, "if the Parks Board had only the right viewpoint they would tender the writer a vote of thanks for furnishing so much ground for so many years for nothing and compliment Council in assisting an industry that has expended so much money and furnished so much labour."

Cold Storage brochure c. 1950.

Another dispute erupted at the next council meeting over a request from James for the rebate of his taxes for the year he was constructing the new building. The taxes amounted to $892 but some councillors questioned the legality of cancelling them. The Court of Revision met and voted Mr. James a reduction of $352.

James then asked council for $500 to help defray the expenses involved in setting up the new cold storage, pointing out that if he, or anyone else, had brought a large, new industry to town, tax concessions or grants would be readily made, and council would have "given me a banquet in the Gilbert House."

"I oppose this measure and I oppose it strenuously," said Alderman W.B. McClung, "The cancellation of taxes is illegal." He said it would have been an entirely different matter if James had applied to Council at the time he decided to rebuild, for a change in the assessment. McClung, O. Alyea and W.W. Miller were emphatic in declaring that council could not accede to the request, while Councillors Tom Jarrett and Hubert Strong were in favour. Councillor Alex LaMoore said he would reserve his decision.

Mayor C.W. Lott praised James for the "tremendous good" he had done for the town "in employing the unemployed" during the summer. "Mr. James has done a great deal for the town in bringing this plant to Trenton and it is only right, it is the business thing to do something for him."

The Trent Theatre block, Trenton.

The new plant is, interjected James, "the only ray of sunshine this year and has brought farmers from Brighton, Colborne and other points that previously never came here. This has meant business to the Town of Trenton and this matter of five hundred dollars is a negligible thing when you consider what has been brought here."

On Nov, 19, a motion by Jarrett, seconded by Strong was made to pay James $892.50 "as a grant for his time and expenses in securing the Cold Storage industry for Trenton, provided, however, that such order of the Treasurer be withheld until a legal opinion is obtained as to the legality of such payment to Eben James, and if found to be illegal then this resolution to be of no effect."

Alyea, Jarrett, LaMoore, Miller and Strong voted for the motion, McClung was opposed.

On Nov. 23, council received a letter from Thomas F. Hall, K.C., of Cobourg, saying he had been retained by W.A. Fraser, M.P. to protest against the payment to Evan (sic) James. "If this resolution is acted upon my instructions are to bring proceedings against the Municipal Corporation and the Members of the Council individually whether by way of Injunction to restrain the payment or an action to recover the amount for the Corporation."

A letter to the town clerk from solicitor H.D. Graham of Trenton outlined the provisions of the Assessment Act and the powers of the Court of Revision. He said a council could not, in the absence of express statutory authority make a grant out of corporate funds. "If authority to grant a bonus (or to do any other thing) is lacking, then a By-Law designed to accomplish this end by indirect means is invalid although it is ostensibly one that is within the competence of the Council to enact."

Graham said he concluded the payment to James would be illegal.

The dispute erupted again at the town's nomination meeting in December when the mayor and council were re-elected by acclamation.

Fraser was involved in some of the hot exchanges over both the land deal and the rebatement of taxes.

The audience was delighted with the spirited talk, said the *Courier-Advocate*, which provided a lengthy and colourful report of the proceedings.

"Shades of Themistocles, Demosthenes and other great men of the Ionian Peninsula, came to life in verbal form at the Nomination Meeting conducted in the Town Hall," said the newspaper, "Words, reams and reams of words were uttered by the several speakers; words that flowed forth with all the fluency of the silver voiced Pericles were uttered often tingled with warmth and in some cases, a little too much warmth in repartee."

The city hall was packed full and, it was, the writer said, "one of the peppiest and hottest that has ever been conducted in this town in many a year."

And one of the most vocal participants was Fraser, former Mayor, and now the Northumberland Riding M.P., "who has been termed the fighting Irishman and who proved to his fellow citizens in this Town of Trenton that his term in the Dominion Legislature has served in making him a spokesman of the first water."

Opposed to him were James and Councillor Tom Jarrett, "two well-known public figures who have graced many a Trenton platform in years past. They did not mince words these three men and at times the language was not such as is used in Webster's Dictionary, but it was to the point and perhaps the better understood."

Jarrett, in defending the proposal to abate James' taxes, mentioned council had come to a fixed assessment arrangement with Fraser over the Trent Theatre property. "What difference is there between the case of James and that of Fraser?"

Eben James got into "fighting mode" and told of the early days of the apple packing industry, "in which he had taken a prominent part." He said when Capt. Bruce Bairnsfather was here, he had allowed the fledgling Trenton-based film company to use his plant so that it wouldn't go out of Trenton. "I lost $220 by giving them the building and in addition had my taxes raised from a $5,000 to $10,000 basis of assessment."

In any event, James was back in the cold storage business and had, by this time, given up his attempts to either convert the building to a distillery or to sell the property. A 3-column newspaper advertisement informed local apple

What the

Trenton

Cold Storage

Means to the

APPLE GROWER

1   The building of the most modern Cold Storage Plant in this district, operated principally for handling apples, has increased the value of every cultivated orchard within its radius to an extent hard to estimate.

2   A new era has arrived for the apple grower, an opportunity he never had before, to get higher market price for his produce, with most of the worry eliminated.

3   Growers and dealers, who used this Storage last season, made around $25,000.00 by expert packing, storing and marketing above prices obtainable at picking time and using old-fashioned methods.

4   Canadian and United States crops are all considerably below 1931, when high prices were paid for cold stored apples held for markets.

5   The increased price received for expertly graded and stored fruit (brand already established) should pay far more than the entire cost of grading and storing. It did last year and should every year.

Apples were trucked from Newcastle district for 15c per barrel last season. Deducting the saving on eastern freight the net cost to the grower from orchard to storage was 5c per barrel.

Cover of four-page brochure distributed in September, 1932.

growers that the cold storage was back in business and invited them to order the space they required "to avoid disappointment."

The federal grant was still not settled by January, 1932, Tummon informing James that the problem was not with the Agricultural Branch but with the Auditor-General who had "taken exception" to the payment of a grant on already existing or previous construction. "It does not affect you alone but other cold storage plants as well." Such payments have been made for years, Tummon said, "and it is only within the last four or five months that the question has been raised."

Tummon said it might be necessary for the Agricultural Branch to refer the matter to the Justice Department, whose ruling would be final.

"After talking to Fraser, I went and seen (sic) personally the Deputy Minister of Justice. Guthrie is taking an interest in the matter, as he has some one affected also, just as you are. The Deputy thinks the merit is all on the side of the Agriculture Branch, but says, of course, he does not know what view the Law officers of the Crown will take."

Tummon said Fraser told him he had phoned James "as he was trying to satisfy the Auditor General's Department."

Fraser, who telephoned and wrote James about the progress of the grant application appeared, on the surface, to be attempting to help a constituent in any way he could, but the old antagonisms from the cooperage business arguments were still in evidence.

The marriage of his sister, Jeanie, to James, although it was a very satisfactory relationship for both, still rankled with Fraser and he was also a bitter political foe of James, who was president of the local Conservative Party.

James, of course, knew what the problem was in Ottawa and wrote to Tummon on Jan, 27, 1932 to thank him for his work. "I do not know whether this is a result of some of our political opponents, but it looks suspiciously like it to me."

The government has always understood, he said, that cold storage facilities needed public support, they "did not usually pay, hence the support given them under the Act and under the Act, very few have been built – in fact, hardly any until the Ontario or other local Government granted financial assistance."

"As you say, it may be necessary to change the Act – in the meantime. I am gasping for breath financially and if a recommendation could be made to the Auditor General to give us our payment pending the decision of the High Court informing him that the Act will be changed to make it legal, it would help me a great deal."

James added a postscript: "Some of our political opponents are naturally very anxious to get me in a jam, which cannot be allowed. This Storage has gone over big this year and promises bigger things in the future."

CHAPTER 15

Political Campaigns

The fractious relationship between Eben James and Bill Fraser was to continue throughout James' life. Although it had started with the conflict over the cooperage mill and Fraser's uncontrollable anger over James' relationship with his sister, Jeanie, it reached a climax over political considerations.

James was the president of the Trenton Conservative Association and Fraser was a Liberal who was to become the Member of Parliament for Northumberland Riding. In 1917, James and Fraser had both supported Liberal R. J. Graham of Belleville, who owned an apple evaporating plant, in his attempt to unseat the Conservative member, E. Guss Porter. Graham lost but told James that, although disappointed, he preferred defeat to success "with the methods adopted by our opponents."

In August, 1926, Fraser, who was then Mayor of Trenton, was tendered an unanimous nomination at the Liberal Convention held in Warkworth, for Northumberland Riding. "Obviously it was a Fraser meeting," reported the *Quinte Sun*, "and the prospective candidate responded with a stirring speech, frequently interrupted by applause and laughter, that suggested a formidable opponent for the Conservative standard-bearer, Milton E. Maybee."

Fraser did not accept the nomination immediately but asked for a week to consider the offer, and to organize his business affairs. He said he was a farmer and lived just 100 yards from the Northumberland boundary. "I'm interested in the canning industry in Northumberland and I have warehouses and cooper shops throughout the county."

James, writing to Poupart said a Dominion election was underway and that he was "up to his eyes" in work, as president of the local Conservative Association. "I have a big scheme in view regarding handling of fruit which includes a large timber limit in Northern Ontario and it is of the utmost importance that I make a good showing at the election."

"Am out speaking two or three nights a week in the surrounding district and have not been able to give the time to this apple business that I would have liked but it will soon be over. We are doing our best to oust the King Government which in my humble opinion means a great deal to the future of this country."

In the meantime, he said, he had from five to eight hundred barrels of apples to send to Glasgow as well as a big shipment to Hull.

Front Street CPR bridge

James wrote a number of drafts for press releases attacking Fraser. He claimed Fraser had formed a combine with other Canadian cooperage manufacturers to keep up the price of cooperage and barrels, "even to reading the riot act, to any small coopers who would not keep the price up."

He referred to a comment Fraser had made about "tin horn Tories who wore uniforms," a reference to James' militia service. James observed it "may not be generally known but the militia records will show that he (Fraser) was for a short time a lieutenant during the war and surely (he) could have been spared as well as many others who left not only a wife but a family of children." James claimed Fraser "preferred (instead of military service) to profit in the manufacture of munition boxes and sell material for erecting the munitions plant at Trenton which was much more profitable."

The bitterness James felt about Fraser becomes obvious when he continued, "Even as Mayor, his greedy and grasping instinct gets the better of him."

"Frasers supreme god is money, the finer instincts that govern most men in acquiring it are quite lacking in him."

These draft press releases found in the James papers, may not have been published in this form, however, or they would most certainly have led to a suit from the litigious Fraser.

Fraser did not get elected on this occasion and he laid some of the blame on James. He did, in fact, claim James and his supporters had libelled him and he began an action against James in Hastings County, and against Gordon R. Sheppard of Toronto in York County Court.

Copies of the Statutory Declarations made by both James and Sheppard are found in James' personal papers. They are dated September, 1928 but it is not known if they were, in fact, ever signed or sworn to.

Fraser had objected to remarks James had allegedly made about his personal and business life and, in particular, comments made about Fraser's opposition to James plans for a distillery. Sheppard, speaking at a public meeting, had allegedly claimed Fraser had made money out of bootlegging.

While James had used strong words at political meetings to describe Fraser, his opponent had been no friendlier. Eben James II recalled Fraser once describing his father as "a Church of England, imperialistic Tory."

Fraser was elected as Member of Parliament for Northumberland Riding in 1930, and again in 1935 and 1940, serving to 1945. He was Chairman of the Public Accounts Committee for 10 years. Fraser was summoned to the Senate on June 25, 1949.

Who's Who in Canada, 1960-61, describes Fraser as an industrialist. He was a director of the Lord Simcoe Hotel, Toronto and the Lord Elgin Hotel, Ottawa, in addition to his extensive Trenton business interests. Born on April 24, 1886, he died on Oct. 26, 1962.

Senator W.A. Fraser

In his later years, Fraser frequently claimed that he had been the founder of the Trenton Cooperage Mill. A tribute to him by the Hon. Lionel Choquette printed in the Debates of the Senate for Tuesday, Oct. 30, 1962, repeats this claim of Frasers. The Hon. W. Ross Macdonald, in his tribute, described Fraser as being a man of strong views, with "strong likes and dislikes."

A local editorial on "Billy Fraser" said that much of the boisterous vigour of his younger days had died in later life, "though as a man he did not appear to mellow much with passing time."

Fraser remained vindictive towards his former Cooperage Mill partner, Eben James, despite the happiness his brother-in-law had provided to his sister, Jeanie. After James' death, however, he rallied to the support of James' son, Eben II who, at a young age, had taken on the burden of managing Trenton Cold Storage.

"The Senator appeared to repent of his treatment of my father after the old man had gone. He frequently expressed his regret to me about past events," said Eben II.

Although Fraser was willing to help his nephew, he was ever the businessman and his help, at times, had conditions attached. Nevertheless, over the years, James and his uncle built up a close, strong and friendly relationship.

CHAPTER 16

Wartime Work

The export of apples came to a halt at the start of the Second World War. Even if shipping had been available, the Cold Storage plant could not continue in the fruit business. The Dominion Department of Agriculture, under the War Measures Act, required the company to turn to activities that would support the war effort. The company was ordered to become involved in the production, storage and shipping of dried egg powder destined for Great Britain.

Fresh eggs, transported by rail in ice-refrigerated reefer cars, arrived at the plant daily from all over Canada. James can recall seeing as many as 100 rail cars loaded with eggs waiting to be unloaded. These eggs were broken and the contents made into a "melange." Some 150 to 200 women were employed breaking the eggs by hand. This melange, was moved in stainless steel drums, to the Canada Doughnut Company Ltd., plant located on Dufferin Street, Trenton, where it was dried, the powder being packed in 20-pound wax-coated cases for overseas shipment.

R.H. Haker, vice-president and director of manufacturing for the Canada Doughnut Company recalling the war years in March, 1957 at a time when the company was installing new automatic machinery, said the company had dried 36,000 eggs a day in a round-the-clock operation during the war.

This activity continued through the war and for several years afterwards, ending around 1950 after the post-war demand for dried eggs from England stopped.

At this time, a number of storage lockers were also available at the cold storage for rent by businesses and individuals.

Some of the cold storage permanent and part-time staff had joined the military. Three brothers of George Frauts, who worked at the storage plant during the war, served in the Royal Canadian Air Force.

Clarence Frauts died when his aircraft crashed over Germany in 1944. He was 25 years old. Jack Frauts, survived the war but was a Prisoner of War during 1944-45.

Bill Frauts, the youngest of the brothers, born in 1920, also served in the Royal Canadian Air Force.

Clarke Jackson, whose father, Art Jackson, was the Chief Engineer at the plant for 35 years, served as a wireless operator with the Lake Superior Regiment. He was wounded in Holland on March 7, 1945 and died on March 14, 1945. He was 21 years old.

Art Jackson's wife, Vera, also worked as a forewoman during the years that eggs were broken and prepared to be dried for shipment overseas in powdered form. Their son, Clarke, had worked in the plant as a boy during summer school holidays, as did another son, Bernie.

In 1950, it became necessary to find alternative uses for the building, which had deteriorated badly during the war years. The apple export business was finished. Britain's own apple production had dramatically increased and supplies were also reaching the United Kingdom from other countries.

The most promising business for the plant appeared to be frozen vegetables as well as grading and storing Cheddar cheese for the Belleville Cheddar Cheese Company (a company started by Bob Hart, later re-named Black Diamond Cheese). Curing rooms were added to the building to enable cheese to age. Some apples were graded and stored in Cold Atmosphere rooms for North American distribution.

Clarence Frauts

A decline in the demand for cheese for export, forced Trenton Cold Storage to look for new customers, and these included Baxter Canning Company of Bloomfield, Canadian Canners and Stokely Van Camp. Trenton Cold Storage grew rapidly as consumer demand for frozen foods increased.

Trenton Cold Storage began negotiations in 1953 with Canadian Canners to build a freezing operation for retail packaging and bulk peas. In the winter and spring of 1954, a Finnegan freezer was installed to look after the freezing of Canadian Canners bulk peas and the following year, four large plate freezers were installed to freeze their retail packages. This production came from their plant in Frankford, Ontario. In 1956, Canadian Canners was taken over by the California Packing Company (Del Monte) who were not involved in the frozen vegetable business in the United States and who phased out their frozen vegetable business in Canada in 1962.

Clarke Jackson

The contract that had originally been made with Canadian Canners ran until 1964 and Trenton Cold Storage were able to purchase their pea processing equipment along with their retail packaging equipment and this was installed at the Trenton Cold Storage plant.

The company was now able to contract for the processing and freezing of peas directly from the combines. Baxter Canning Company and Omar Farms were both bringing peas to Trenton to be processed, frozen and packaged. Stokely's was also bringing peas and cut corn to be frozen and packaged.

"The closing out of Canadian Canners turned out to be a blessing in disguise because we were able to process and freeze for a number of grower organizations," said James. The Provincial government was tightening the environmental laws and it became apparent in 1970 that it would no longer

Trenton Cold Storage buildings, c. 1950.

be possible to process peas in downtown Trenton. This also affected the Stokely Van Camp Company whose plant was located in downtown Trenton on the shores of the Bay of Quinte.

Stokely's announced in the spring of 1970 that they would not be processing anything at their Trenton plant after that season, a matter of great concern to the farmers of this area. Del Monte had closed out all of their small plants in Eastern Ontario and now the Stokely Van Camp plant was closing out.

By the early 1950's, the plant was completely into low temperature refrigeration. But keeping things going during the fifties and sixties proved difficult, even with Fraser's help, James admits. "We did not have a long-term plan in those days but we grew. If my father had been around to see the growth over those years he would have been amazed. Fraser would also have found it difficult to believe what we managed to achieve in the 1970's."

The cold storage business was continually changing. Consumers were increasingly buying frozen products, including prepared dinners as well as packages of frozen vegetables. James said the time came when the company had to change its business stance to remain viable.

"We started looking for businesses that could use our services and contracted with a number of companies to package and store their products. We worked with farmers in processing and packaging their vegetables."

"Things came to a zenith and then began to fall off again," James said. "We needed to find something new. At that time companies were looking to other companies to provide specialized services in the distribution of frozen products."

The company's fortunes began to improve when contracts were negotiated with Quaker Oats Company who were manufacturing frozen waffles and, later, French toast and muffin mix. Quaker had earlier used the cold storage facilities to store pet food ingredients for their new Trenton plant. Frozen bakery products were also being stored.

"Over the years my father had to continually find new things to do to keep the plant operating and so did I," James said. He recalled that in the last few years of his father's life the pair would argue heatedly over changes in the market place and what needed to be done to stay in business.

"Mother would intercede when the arguments got too hot. Father would eventually insist that things be done his way 'as long as he was here'. If I wanted to wreck the place," he said, "I would have to do it after he was gone. He said he was the one that signed the cheques! And he continued to do so until the day he drew his last breath."

Mawnan (Babe) was undecided about coming into the business. Babe had been attending Trinity College, Port Hope, leaving school the year after their father had died. "He was the baby of the family and, I think, my mother's favourite child. He was very musical, I recall. Some discussion took place about him going into the hardware business."

Babe attended Albert College in Belleville taking a business course before he decided to join the firm. He worked in the shipping office and also showed considerable aptitude for anything mechanical.

"I was an average student, although I had a lot of 'attitude'," Eben James said. "I had many hobbies. I built boats and did things with my hands. My father worked with me making things. I had a close relationship with my father. He bought me a sailboat when I was young and taught me sailing. He also bought me an ice boat, took me duck and pheasant hunting, taught me to ride a horse and rode with me — English saddle, of course."

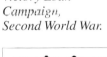

Victory Loan Campaign, Second World War.

James father was older than all the fathers of his friends.

"He also wore a prominent moustache which was not in vogue in those days. He had a full head of hair and was always well dressed – his clothes were mostly bought in England. He never came to the office without a jacket and usually wore a suit. He died when I was very young. I would have liked to have known him better."

James said his father was well read, always positive and always upbeat. He instilled in his son the determination to succeed even when things were not going well.

"Mother's purpose in life was to do her best for her husband and children. When father was sick over a three or four year period and spending a great deal of time in hospital in Kingston, she would stay down there and watch over him, like a private nurse or more so. My mother, who was 17 years younger than my father, was devoted to him."

His father had prostate cancer and serious heart problems. James recalls his mother telling him of a man next door with similar problems who had been admitted to hospital in Kingston and who had never returned home.

"She was trying to prepare me for what would be taking place. After my

*Canadian Doughnut
Company, Ltd.
letterhead.*

father died I spent a lot of time with my uncle, Bill Fraser, who was then a Senator. Fraser was a pugnacious street fighter and maybe some of these traits rubbed off on me. Some people would go after me because of my uncle. I grew up ducking."

By the 1970's, James had developed more confidence in business dealings and a greater "presence" in the community. He had attended boarding school at St. Andrew's, Aurora, for a short period before changing to Albert College in Belleville to enter his Commerce course. He had not been well received by the "old-timers" at the plant when he first began working in the company office.

"I did everything in those days. I worked in the office, in the plant, and learned to run the compressor plant. After my father died I asked the old-timers to work with me and they did – previously (because he was the proprietor's son) they often made things tough for me. The clerk at that time was Arthur Salisbury who had been here a long time."

"The company was not a major one in those days. We started to move when we built the waffle plant adjacent to our plant for Quaker Oats in 1966-67."

CHAPTER 17

Produce Processors

E ben James I had a business relationship with Clayton Metcalfe's father, Elwood, in 1936, and installed specialized freezing equipment to freeze peas, in round cylinder containers, which Metcalfe was processing in Deseronto, Ont. This was the beginning of the frozen food industry for Trenton Cold Storage.

It had only been a few years before this that Clarence Birdseye* (1886-1956) a businessman and inventor, born in New York, had developed a process for freezing food in small packages suitable for retailing. Elwood Metcalfe brought the idea to this area. Unfortunately, he died, prematurely, in May, 1937, and nothing further took place in the frozen vegetable business until after the war.

Various Canadian soup companies were developing the use of frozen vegetables in their mixes for their vegetable soups. In the past, they had used vegetables from brine but the frozen vegetables gave a better appearance and an improved quality to their product.

One major company entered into a buying contract with Clayton Metcalfe, Elwood's son. Clayton asked Trenton Cold Storage to do the freezing of peas, and later, corn and beans. The big soup company that Metcalfe was dealing with was a large volume buyer of frozen vegetables before the retail market was launched. Many people were buying refrigerators with larger frozen food compartments and this accelerated the consumption of frozen vegetables.

The business of freezing Metcalfe's products for the soup company had developed to a large volume when the company said they wanted the product frozen where it was processed. So, Metcalfe, with financial assistance from the company, installed freezing facilities at their Deseronto plant. This impacted on Trenton Cold Storage and it became necessary for them to find new customers.

"We approached the Stokely Van Camp Company of Canada, which had a large processing facility near our cold storage plant, to pick up the excess capacity that we found we now had" said James.

"I worked with Bill Miskamin (President of Stokely's) and Clayton Maxwell (sales manager) to develop sales for our unused capacity. The Stokely

---

* He founded the General Seafoods Company in 1924, later becoming president of Birdseye Frosted Foods (1930-34). Some 300 patents are credited to him, from infra-red heat lamps to the process for removing water from food.

Eben II at school

people and Trenton Cold Storage were very successful in building this volume and Stokely's export office also developed sales in the United Kingdom, a country that had not then reached its full potential in the frozen vegetable business. In later years, when the pea harvest did not materialize, we were importing frozen peas from the U.K., as it had become a very large producer of frozen peas."

In the early 1950's, vegetable-processing facilities did not have sewage disposal plants and they would dispose of their waste effluent in the streams or lakes where they were located. The Ontario government was requiring municipalities to improve their own sewage disposal systems as, in most cases, the systems were not large enough to accommodate the effluent from vegetable processing facilities.

As a result, Stokely's were forced to either spend millions of dollars on their own sewage system or close out their Trenton operation. They chose to move the production from their Trenton plant to their Whitby plant. This was in the early 1970's.

Bill Oosterink, an apple grower and farmer from the Brighton area, the owner of Omar Farm Produce Ltd., had been growing and harvesting peas and bringing them to Trenton Cold Storage for freezing and packaging. He, along with the Stokely growers and harvesters, approached the Minister of Agriculture, William Stewart, about the plight of the vegetable growers in Eastern Ontario, asking him for assistance.

Oosterink got permission from the ministry to lease the Stokely's Trenton plant for one season, with the understanding that the growers would have to find alternative processing facilities the next year. Oosterink and the growers did a very good job in growing and processing peas in the Stokely plant that year and Oosterink found sales for this total production. He was a contractor to the growers.

PRODUCE PROCESSORS LIMITED

After the season was over, James received a telephone call from Herb Crown who was the Director of the ARDA (Agriculture Rehabilitation Development Agency) branch of the Ontario Ministry of Agriculture.

"He asked me to come to Toronto to meet with him and his department heads to discuss the future of the vegetable processing and freezing industry in Eastern Ontario. It should be mentioned here that the new sewage regulations that had come down from the Ontario Water Resources Commision had the effect of closing out many of the small processors from Shannonville to Bowmanville, as well as in and around Prince Edward County. The Minister of Agriculture was concerned that this part of agriculture would cease to exist in an area that had been in the forefront of the canning and vegetable industry of the province.

"It was Clayton Metcalfe and his father who were one of the founders of the Ontario Food Processors Association," James said.

Mr. Crown told James that the Minister wanted to keep the Eastern Ontario vegetable industry alive. Since Trenton Cold Storage was processing, freezing and packaging, and also custom freezing, for Stokely's, Oosterkink and the growers, he suggested TCS should become involved in the establishment of a new processing facility where the wastewater could be sprayed on farm fields.

The new facility was to be known as Produce Processors Limited. It would have shareholders who would be growers and harvesters. Oosterink would be the contractor looking after the marketing of the product and Trenton Cold Storage would provide the freezing, warehousing and packaging components.

"After meeting with the Minister, I said I would talk to my brother (Babe) and then get back to him. The Minister also informed me before I left that day that I would have to act as President of the company without personal remuneration as we would continue to do the freezing, packaging and warehousing of the finished product. I believe the minister's words were to the effect that when the government turns over large sums of money to the farmers, disagreements could be expected in the future. The minister said, the government did not want any grounds to have the Opposition claim the government had wasted taxpayer's money."

James discussed the proposal with Babe.

"We felt that we had nothing to lose. We were young and prepared to accept the challenge. The property that was chosen was sandy, ideal for

Processing corn at Produce Processor Limited.

spraying wastewater and had a supply of water nearby." This property belonged to the W.A. Fraser estate, which was being managed by the Guaranty Trust Company of Canada. As co-executor of the estate, James approached the trust company's president, Alan Ramsey, about the possibility of selling off 70 acres of this land to this new incorporated body, made up of just over 30 shareholders.

The trust company agreed to this proposal provided that a number of independent valuations were made of the land. An agreement was reached and the ARDA branch agreed to provide $150,000 on a $370,000 budget. The shareholders were to provide the remainder of the money.

Oosterink was the contractor so he would be financing the growing, harvesting and processing of the crop. Oosterink was confident that he could handle this part of the arrangement.

"Babe worked with his friends in the food processing industry and the food machinery people to come up with a pea line and a corn line and the number of square feet required to accommodate this facility. The freezing and warehousing would be carried out at the downtown plant as it had been in the past. By the time these arrangements were completed, it was February and Babe moved in on a frozen field, laid out the facility, getting the plant built, and began installing equipment to process the peas and corn in July, August and September.

"Babe was the genius behind the Produce Processors operation. He built two processing lines, one for peas and one for corn, not only operating it but producing a product that we were able to sell in the local market and also to export to the U.K. What he was able to do in providing a large volume of treated water and the waste disposal would be major hurdles for even a large company."

For a couple of country boys the creation of Produce Processors was an outstanding feat.

Buyers from the United Kingdom arrived in Ontario to inspect the facility. They said they were prepared to import Ontario grown corn but that it had to be frozen where it was processed.

"We were put in a position requiring us to move the freezing lines, compressor plant and hydro transformer systems to the new processing facility on Telephone Road, This became a very expensive project and, of course, as we owned the freezing facility it was our financial responsibility."

James said Trenton Cold Storage entered into an arrangement with Produce Processors Limited to lease sufficient space to install equipment and the compressor plant so that the entire manufacturing process was carried out at one location.

"Oosterink was exporting to the European Economic Community and he had to meet their standards and that required the investment of hundreds of thousands of dollars in equipment in the corn line."

The ARDA branch of the Ministry of Agriculture was not prepared to advance any more money and it was necessary for the shareholders, the growers and harvesters to provide the capital.

"The ARDA branch conducted the meetings, the farmers attended and a few agreed to buy additional shares but most declined to do so. Babe and I were in a position where we had also made large capital outlays to move and install the freezing system at the processing facility. But if the plant could not get EEC approval, much of the corn production would be lost."

The James family were in the warehousing business. The food processing business, over the years, provided volume to their freezing facilities, which in turn helped fill their warehouses.

"We were not vegetable processors; we had followed a policy of servicing other industries that required fast freezing, low temperature warehousing, packaging and distribution. We were now being forced to come forward with large sums of capital to keep the facility going. Babe James had built an excellent facility; he had continued to study operations around North America, bringing the best ideas that he found back to Trenton. We found that we were using our energies away from our known business; we did not like it, but we did not feel we had any choice."

While this was taking place, the multi-nationals who operated on thousands of acres of their own farms, or farms they controlled, were undercutting Oosterink, the growers' contractor. The Ontario Vegetable Growers Marketing Board, in conjunction with the processors negotiating committee, established the prices each year for all vegetable crops. The large operators were not as concerned if the price of corn went up affecting export market sales, because they were also growers and were more able to adjust to the price changes.

Oosterink informed the growers that he could no longer meet the marketing board price for export corn. He said, if they wanted their acreage sold, they had to be prepared to accept less than the negotiated price under the regulations of the Farm Products Marketing Board. The growers were prepared to do this and so they continued to grow a large acreage that year. Oosterink paid them approximately $10 per ton less than the marketing board price and his export market continued to grow.

William G. Norman succeeded William Stewart as Ontario Minister of Agriculture in 1975. The marketing board, at this time, took issue with what was taking place in Eastern Ontario and demanded that the new minister bring the matter to a head. A meeting was held in the Ministry's boardroom, where the Ontario Vegetable Growers Marketing Board members and Omar Farm Produce growers representatives met. Eben James was present.

"The Minister pointed out to the marketing board people, many of them from Southwestern Ontario, that he had growers in Eastern Ontario who were not only prepared to grow corn, but were prepared to grow corn for export and accept less money than the marketing board had negotiated. He said he did not wish to put these one hundred, or more, growers out of business."

Arising from this meeting, a co-operative was proposed – to be called the Eastern Ontario Vegetable Growers Co-operative. They were to undertake the contracting, harvesting and marketing. Oosterink, who had been doing this, agreed to work with the co-operative in selling their crops. The co-operative entered into negotiations with the Bank of Montreal to look after their account and the bank provided them with the money necessary to take their product from the field to the marketplace.

The export market price was negotiated with the marketing board on a two-price system – one for domestic and one for export.

"Things went along reasonably well until the marketing board decided to narrow the pricing between the domestic market and the export market. At this point, the marketing board was told by the Eastern Ontario growers that they were determined to survive and said if the board did not maintain the spread between the domestic and export prices of corn, then the co-operative intended to contravene the marketing board act."

James was asked to sit on the negotiating team with the processors to establish the price of sweet corn. He found himself to be in very unfriendly territory.

"It became apparent to me that the large packers who possessed the clout at these negotiations were not really concerned about the price of export corn and, of course, with their integrated acreage, they did not have to be. I was not a bit backward in pointing out to them that we gave the process credibility because we were on marginal land in Eastern Ontario with less heat units than Central and Southwestern Ontario."

James suggested it would be in the best interests of the large packers not to be perceived as responsible for putting the smaller Eastern Ontario growers out of business.

"I do not believe the marketing board people ever showed too much sympathy for the growers in the east. If you look at the acreage today, I don't believe the marketing board has any representatives on the pea and corn negotiations anywhere east of Toronto."

While all this was taking place, Israeli buyers came to visit the plant. They had built plants in Israel using irrigated land, had preferential treatment and leverage in the EEC countries. Competition for the overseas market had become cut-throat.

The free trade arrangements in Canada were also taking effect and all these factors brought pressure on Trenton Cold Storage to give back discounts on the freezing and storage to growers when, at the end of the year, they were unable to meet their bank obligations. During this time a number of additions had been built on to the processing plant – packaging lines had been upgraded and modernized; the cob line had doubled in capacity and these costs had been born, in the main, by Trenton Cold Storage.

CHAPTER 18

Eben James III joins TCS

After completing his MBA degree at York University, Eben James III took a summer job at Trenton Cold Storage. He intended, however, to seek employment in Toronto in the fall.

Eben III worked next to Andy Laufer who had recently been engaged as Company Controller. Laufer had come to Trenton Cold Storage from Peterborough in February and his family was intending to move to Trenton when school was out. Laufer told Eben James in June that the family preferred to stay in Peterborough, therefore he had found a new position in that city.

Laufer appraised James of the situation at Trenton Cold Storage as he saw it and James asked him who he could hire as a Controller. Laufer strongly recommended Eben Junior, observing he had a comprehensive knowledge of the operation and was, in his opinion, the best person for the job.

About this time Eben Jr. told his father that he had received a telephone call from the H.P. Hood Company in Boston (a company for which Trenton Cold Storage was co-packing juice) offering him an interview for a job in their marketing department.

"He asked me how I felt about it. I told him that I was over 60 years of age, and my brother, Babe, was taking less interest in the business, a situation that had been of concern to me. I said that if he did not join the company it might be necessary to put the family-owned operation on the market in the future."

Eben Jr. agreed to stay at Trenton Cold Storage and accept the position of Controller, with the understanding that he was to be completely responsible for the company's financial planning.

"He was just the person at the right time for this job. Eben Jr. had grown up in the country where the conversation around the dinner table in the evening was about business. From early on, he had developed a keen understanding of the Company's financial affairs. He expressed concern, however, about the lack of budgets and controls."

Over and above his financial ability, Eben Jr. understood the plant's operation. He had worked, for many years, at the plant during the summer months. He had taken his engineer's papers before he was 16 and his relationship with the staff was good.

One of the first things that Eben Jr. brought to his father's attention was the inadvisability of giving very large discounts to the Co-operative to enable them to meet their financial commitments with their bank.

"He said, we have our budgets and apparently they have theirs, but we will no longer be finishing off the year using warehousing revenue in order for them to continue in business. This is no longer acceptable."

James agreed that the practice of providing discounts should be stopped.

Eben III prepared budgets for the companies in the TCS Group.

"Everyone had a part in the preparation of the budgets. They were analyzed, checked and agreed to and everyone was expected to live within their budgets. The Co-operative was not quite so demanding of itself and when it came to a shortfall, Eben would not agree to TCS covering it. Despite this, the bank continued to support them. Over a period of time, however, it became apparent to Eben Jr. that we should start to reserve for this doubtful account – one pertaining to the processing revenue and the other the warehousing revenue."

In 1990, Eben III told his father that the Royal Bank of Canada had offered them a very attractive business relationship. Bank officials had studied the financial statements of the processing, freezing and warehousing operations and were interested in the account. Eben recommended moving the processing account to that bank because, at that time, the TCS Group and the Co-operative were using the same lender, the Bank of Montreal. He felt this was unwise.

Eben III also earmarked $1.5 million as a "doubtful account" against the Co-operative in the company's books. He was afraid they would go into receivership if they continued to operate in their present manner.

"We had had a long relationship with the Bank of Montreal," said Eben II. "My grandfather, Robert Alexander Fraser, was manager of the Molson's Bank in the 1880's when it was taken over by the Bank of Montreal. The Bank of Montreal had held a mini-board meeting in Trenton in 1980 to mark their 100th anniversary. Present at a luncheon were the grandsons of Robert Fraser – Robin Fraser of Fraser Beatty, Donald Fraser of Loyalist College, M.F. (Babe) James, and myself."

"The minutes of the transactions made by Robert Fraser one hundred years earlier were read. Those present were all presented with framed drawings of the downtown Trenton branch of the bank. The directors of the bank were very kind and very complimentary to the grandsons, particularly to Babe and myself, for the long and rewarding relationship between the Bank and the TCS group. They said it was an outstanding occasion for the Bank to have the four grandsons of the original manager, one hundred years ago, present at the luncheon with the board of directors and key executives of the Bank of Montreal."

Because of this long relationship, Eben James II told his son, he felt he must remain loyal to the bank. While the Co-operative may be headed for trouble, James was sure this would not impact on the long and profitable relationship the bank had enjoyed with Trenton Cold Storage, the James brothers and their uncle, Senator Bill Fraser.

"The decision was mine, Junior told me, but he added he would still feel more comfortable if the account was moved," James said.

While $1.5 million had been set aside by Trenton Cold Storage as a

Eben W.O. James III

"doubtful account" reserve by 1993 it had become apparent to the bank that some action would be necessary regarding the Co operative account.

"I was in the Holy Land that May, following a warehousing convention that had been held in the Middle East, when I received a call from Eben Jr. to tell me that the bank had moved on the Co-operative. They had brought in a receiver and were moving on the inventory which was in the range of $10-million plus."

Eben Jr. had the inventory covered under the Warehousemen's Lien Act and asked the bank for a meeting to discuss the monies that were owed to the TCS Group, approximately $2 million.

"The bank said the money was theirs and they wanted it and claimed we had no lien on the inventory. I received another call a few days later from Eben Jr. to say that the bank had gone to the courts but the courts were not prepared to hear arguments on the Warehousemen's Lien Act at that time, and that all monies were to be paid into the court."

In the meantime, the jobs of more than 50 people who had been employed with the processing and packaging organization were in jeopardy because of the demise of the Eastern Ontario Vegetable Growers Co-operative.

Various harvesters and truckers, along with a large number of the growers wanted to salvage the business, however, and asked Eben Jr. if a way to continue processing vegetables could be found.

"Junior telephoned me and said he felt we had to look after the people that had been with the processing facility. The growers and harvesters had agreed to be paid when the product was sold and the money collected. If we agreed to the same terms, they wanted to keep the operation running."

James had some concerns about the proposal but agreed to it. When he arrived back in Trenton he found that the growers had not only located seed, which normally has to be purchased a year in advance, but they had also planted more than 2,000 acres and were securing markets for the coming year's production.

"In July, I received a call at home around 8:30 p.m. from Bob Crease saying that he was from the Bank of Montreal and he would like to meet with us on the following Wednesday at 10 a.m. I asked him what the meeting was about. He said it was to discuss our year-end financial statement which was completed on June 30th. He said he also wished to discuss our budgets for the coming year."

James said some of his financial people were on holiday and asked if another day could be set for the meeting. Crease insisted the meeting must be held on the date and at the time he had indicated.

Crease and another man arrived on the scheduled day and time at the boardroom of Produce Processors, Ltd. Also present were the Produce Processors Ltd. directors.

"I learned at this first meeting that I had had a long relationship with Crease's father, Douglas, who had been General Manager of the Guaranty Trust Company. They had been executors of the Senator William Fraser estate. I was co-executor along with the senator's lifelong secretary, James Cox. (The trust company had withheld funds from the beneficiary of the Senator Fraser estate which took James some years to have returned to the beneficiary and this result came about after charges were laid by the Department of National Revenue against their president and company)."

Present at the meeting, in addition to Crease and his companion, were Eben James Sr., Eben Jr. and TCS directors Stan Bigford, John Blair and Al Borthwick

The bank representative accompanying Crease bluntly told the assembly that the bank was no longer interested in doing business with the TCS Group. The funds from the sale of the Co-operative inventory were being paid into the courts and, the spokesman said, the bank would not be going to the courts over this matter for five years. In the meantime, he said the bank would no longer support TCS and they wanted their loan paid.

"You could hear a pin drop in the room after this announcement was made. I reminded Mr. Crease and his partner that his phone call had set up this meeting to discuss the financial statements for the year ending June 30th and to discuss the budgets for the coming year. I asked Mr. Crease if there was anything else to discuss at this meeting and he said no. So I adjourned the meeting. But then Crease said they wanted to look over the company's financial statements.

"The financial statement, to say the least, was a surprise to the Bank of Montreal and we were surprised that they had been lending the company millions of dollars and yet appeared to have little knowledge of our operation. They asked us to explain the $750,000 on the Produce Processors Ltd., statement for doubtful accounts. We said the Co-operative owed TCS and PPL more than $2 million in addition to the monies they owed the bank. We showed very favorable year-end balances and it was obvious that this information surprised the bank representatives. We also reserved $750,000 in the TCS statement for doubtful accounts for monies owed on storage.

The two men excused themselves and left to telephone their head office from their local branch. Returning they asked further questions about the financial statements and the operation of the TCS Group. They asked if they could inspect the facilities and Eben James Sr. drove them around the various properties and the farm overlooking the processing plant.

"They asked how many acres we had at the farm and I told them over 1,000 acres. They observed the land was valued in the company books at $47,000 but they considered it was, in fact, worth millions of dollars. I explained the $47,000 figure was what it was valued at when it was first taken onto the books and that was the value at which it was left."

When the group returned to the downtown office they wanted to know what Eben James thought about the bank continuing on as the lender.

"I suggested to them that their supervisor had already made that decision. The eggs had been scrambled, I said, after 100 years of mutually satisfactory business and there was no way to put it back. I told them that we would be looking for a new lender but warned them they were not to withdraw our day to day operating account. We were not asking them to lend us any more money. We had never missed a payment and we had never been late."

The bank representative said it appeared mistakes had been made. The TCS group was a good, sound company with good facilities and, physically and financially, was well run.

"Eben Jr. was waiting for me when I returned to the office and I told him what had taken place. These fellows did not want to lose the account but, as far as we were concerned, our confidence in them was gone. Junior did not remind me that he had advised me three years earlier to move the processing account to the Royal Bank. He was concerned that the loyalty I perceived would not withstand the management record of the Co-operative. When it became apparent to these people that their supervisors were not going to change their minds, their attitude to Eben Jr. and myself remained friendly and cordial."

And as the TCS Group looked for a lawyer to handle the dispute with the Bank over the $2 million covered under the Warehousemen's Lien Act, the Provincial Attorney General announced he would be supporting TCS in the action under the Act against the bank.

The Bank officials must have had second thoughts about the proposed action after the provincial Attorney General entered the picture and they decided to meet with us to discuss the $2 million owing to us from the Co-operative.

"When the whole matter was over, I wrote to the Bank of Montreal president, outlining the James family connection with the Bank for over 100 years, starting with our grandfather, Robert Fraser as manager of the Trenton branch. I reminded him of the anniversary meeting with the board and the reading of minutes of transactions from 100 years earlier. The bank replied cordially, but our relationship was over."

James said he later realized that his son, Eben Jr., had comprehended more clearly the business relationship between the Bank and the Company while his thoughts had been focussed on the long and apparently congenial relationship.

CHAPTER **19**

The Company expands

In the early 1960's, James was looking for additional business to keep his warehouse operation going. He purchased Riverside Dairy from S.O. Graham, intending to amalgamate the dairy with the Cold Storage operation. In those days, milk was still being delivered door-to-door by horse and wagon. He also purchased Trenton Creameries and incorporated this company into the operation.

James ordered new bottling machines and trucks to replace the horses. He did not stay in the dairy business long, however, as Arthur Quickert, manager of Black Diamond Cheese, who stored and aged cheese at TCS, expressed an interest in purchasing the company. Six months later ownership of the dairy changed again when Mr. Quickert purchased the business.

In the early 1960's, TCS had built a relationship with Jim Wharry, President of the Quaker Oats Company. Wharry brought to James' attention, that they were importing frozen waffles from the United States. He wanted to manufacture them in Canada and suggested a joint venture for this production. He made arrangements for the James brothers to visit one of their frozen waffle plants outside the Chicago area. Returning, the brothers met with the Quaker people to develop a manufacturing facility.

A new low temperature warehouse was built in 1966, which was designed to accommodate production of frozen waffles. The following spring, a 14,000 square foot manufacturing plant was built adjacent to this warehouse, for the manufacture of both waffles and French toast. The Quaker Oats Company installed their equipment and managed the operation; Trenton Cold Storage provided the freezing facilities, the low temperature warehouse and distribution services.

Trenton Cold Storage held a dinner at the Royal Canadian Legion in Trenton in the fall of 1967. Mr. Wharry was the guest speaker and area heads of industry and municipal, provincial and federal politicians were invited to welcome the arrival of this new industry. TCS has now had an ongoing relationship with Quaker Oats Company for over 40 years.

Mr. Wharry, a large and very colourful figure and a very entertaining guest speaker, kept the dinner guests interested and amused from the time he began to speak until the evening was over.

About this time, the cold storage plant had been on a manually operated system and Babe felt that the company should move into a sophisticated, automated system. This project was started with a new compressor plant. After the new automated system came on line, the manual system was removed. This new system reduced operating costs and gave more uniform temperatures, which the industry was demanding.

The volume of business was continuing to grow and TCS built additional warehouses.

James was still operating the farm for the Fraser estate. The orchards were upgraded although it was becoming increasingly difficult to market Ontario apples. Glenburnie Farms joined with other area growers to form Quinte Fruit Growers Limited – a facility to store, package and distribute apples to the retail market.

James became a director of this company along with David Zimerman, Walter Rutherford and Andrew Little; Harold Bonter was President.

"I learned some lessons in this venture," recalled James, "it was almost impossible to get the growers to agree on anything and it was only a question of time before they would self destruct. When I was asked to vote on any issue, I used to say: 'Whatever the President and Dr. Zimerman agree on, I will accept.' They agreed to disagree most of the time."

James was invited to become a founding member of the Ontario Apple Marketing Commission, which encompassed all apple-growing districts of the Province. Growers were assessed a fee per acreage and this funded the organization. Its purpose was to promote the sale of Ontario apples. It was felt that anything done to promote Ontario apples would be advantageous. Considerable time was spent at meetings, which were usually held in Toronto at the Food Terminal, where growers discussed, at length, the strengths and weaknesses of the industry.

"After the first year, the growers decided they wanted to set prices. I felt this was not in the best interests of the industry. My thoughts in this regard proved to be correct. The Americans on the south side of Lake Ontario were able to produce apples at a lower cost than we could and there was no duty on apples coming across the border. The policy of setting a price opened up all kinds of avenues for deception. The board would plug one hole and three or four more would develop. In the end it became a disaster."

James had an opportunity to visit Russia in May, before the Iron Curtain came down, and when he returned he found TCS had three rooms of Red Delicious apples, which had not been opened.

"I found that the Ontario Apple Marketing Comission had set a price of $15 per box. Apples were being delivered to the Toronto market from British Columbia and Washington State for $10 per box and there was no way we could be competitive at those prices. Jerry Long was a long-serving chairman of the Ontario Apple Marketing Commission. I called and told him what my problems were. He said he understood, so I asked him what he was going to do about it. Jerry said there was nothing he could do about it. There were seven districts in Ontario, he said and the growers came in once a week. The growers set the price they wanted for their apples and he could not change

This winter scene by artist E. Moshynski is from a company Christmas card. A steam train is on the rail spur and the company sign is high on the roof.

that. I asked what I could do and he said, 'Do what I did; pull your trees out'."

James had spent over $1 million upgrading the orchards with size controlled rootstocks and new varieties, and had more than 330 acres coming into production. It became apparent to him that this was an industry that would be going nowhere.

At the end of the year, Eben III provided the financial statements for the farm operation. More than $250,000 had been lost with no depreciation or management salaries calculated in the equation.

The decision was made to remove the orchards.

One third of all Ontario apples were once grown east of Toronto. Today, there are very few orchards left. Trenton Cold Storage itself had been established many years earlier to market apples overseas.

"It was a great industry at one time but today there is an over production of apples throughout the world. We have areas in California that grow 2,500 to 3,000 boxes per acre. We do well in Ontario if we grow one-half that. The Free Trade Agreement did not bring an even playing field for the agricultural industry."

* * *

The TCS property along Trenton waterfront had a number of water lots and the farm included a large gravel quarry. The decision was made to fill in the water lots and use the gravel in the off season to keep people employed. Over a period of a few years, a 10-acre park was created on the Trenton waterfront.

A few years later, the federal government was offering grants for dredging and breakwaters for marinas along the shores of Lake Ontario and the Bay of Quinte. Cobourg built a beautiful marina. Kingston, Belleville, Gananoque and other communities, some much larger than Trenton, also built marinas. About this time, the City of Trenton engaged Norman Lee, an industrial commissioner, who came from the Pickering area where a marina had proved very successful.

Lee approached Trenton Cold Storage about the possibility of developing

Produce Processors Ltd. official opening dinner programme.

a 150-boat marina. This, he said, would do more to keep downtown Trenton alive than any other enterprise.

"He asked if we would get on side with the City since we had this large block of land extending out into the Bay of Quinte at the mouth of the Trenton-Severn System. I said we would be excited to become part of it and said I could see the day when the cold storage plant would be relocated from the waterfront. Its purpose for being at this location was originally to have access to water transportation, which was no longer a requirement. I said I would like to see the area developed."

Lee asked James to accompany him to a meeting at the Small Harbours Branch in Burlington.

"Both Babe and I had involved ourselves in the local community. I served on Council in 1953; I was President of the Chamber of Commerce, sat on the Court of Revision, and was a member of the Rotary Club. We wanted to see the town grow and improve. This seemed a wonderful opportunity to develop the waterfront."

James and Lee met with officials at the Small Harbours Branch and found they were enthusiastic about developing a marina at the entrance to the Trent-Severn System. The federal government had monies available for breakwaters and dredging.

"George Hees was our Member of Parliament. The only money spent in this Riding had been for a small marina east of the airport. The Provincial government had money available for shore development projects. But the

*Eben James II, Babe
James and (centre)
George Frauts*

Small Harbours Branch was not interested in a 150-boat marina. They wanted one of not less than 350, preferably a 500-boat capacity.

The Small Harbours Branch officials said they would prepare preliminary drawings for the marina.

"Driving back to Trenton, Norm Lee enthused about the project, saying that it was the best thing that could happen to the town. He talked in glowing figures of the amount of money the marina would generate for the area and of the public interest that would be created in the project."

James did not hear from Lee for some weeks, however, and he telephoned to ask what was taking place.

"He said he was working on it. A few months went by. Then Mr. Lee came to my office and announced that he had resigned as Industrial Commissioner of the City of Trenton. He did not wish to burn any bridges, however. He said, it was not what could be done for the community that counted; it was the perception of who was going to gain from this development. He thanked me for all my efforts and time, and left."

* * *

"A few years passed and there was an editorial in the local newspaper about the Waterfront Festival in Belleville remarking on the tens of thousands of dollars it brought to the city. The editor said Trenton should have a marina like Belleville's. I called the editor to tell him that Mr. Lee had tried to develop a marina in Trenton but had run into opposition. The Small Harbours Branch had sent blueprints for a 350-500 boat marina to Trenton, I said, but city officials claimed they had no knowledge of this."

James telephoned the Small Harbours Branch and asked for copies of the plans and these were sent to him.

"I called the city clerk and told him not to bother looking further in the files for the marina plans as I had now obtained them from Burlington. He thanked me for not putting him 'on the spot'."

* * *

In January, 1981, Eben James heard that the H.P. Hood Company, Dunedin, Florida, were looking for a co-packer. Never one to miss an opportunity, James flew to Dunedin, and met with David Bowen, the general manager of the company's citrus operations. Bowen liked the proposals, and officials from the Hood's Boston office visited Trenton later in the year. By October, a new plant had been established in Trenton.

This operation processing orange, apple and cranberry juice from concentrate, continued for many years, eventually being sold to the Coca-Cola Company who still use TCS services.

Also, during this time, FBI Foods were planning to establish a plant to pack juice apples where they could squeeze apples and produce apple juice. The James Brothers arranged for a supply of apples from local growers.

FBI built a new plant in Trenton which operated for many years.

CHAPTER 20

In the newspaper business

When the first venture into vegetable freezing was undertaken, Eben James II found his uncle, Senator Fraser, helpful in arranging for capital and in backing his notes at the bank as well as providing the young man with shrewd advice. Fraser, however, had his own demands. The most challenging of these was when Fraser established The *Trentonian and Tri-County News* newspaper in 1956 and asked James to oversee its operation.

"This was a tremendous challenge," James recalled. "We were getting involved in an industry that we knew nothing about, which was being established in a local area in a local market, totally foreign to anything that I had been involved with in the past. The involvement took me away from the warehousing industry from 1956 through until after the Senator's death in 1963."

For many years, Senator Fraser felt the *Courier-Advocate* had treated him unfairly and that the editor's attacks on him had become personal. J.N. Sisson, who had been a partner of Roy Thompson in Timmins, Ont., came to Trenton and purchased the newspaper. He built his circulation by being strongly critical of Fraser's political and community activities.

Fraser's long-time private secretary, Jimmy Cox, at the Senator's request, had made numerous attempts to purchase the *Courier-Advocate* only to have the offers refused. On each occasion, Sisson predicted that the Senator would return and offer even more money.

In 1955, Cox offered more than $250,000 for the newspaper, which Sisson again refused, telling Cox that Fraser would, within the year, offer even more money. Cox said Fraser would not be making any further offers but would, instead, use the money he had been prepared to offer for the *Courier-Advocate* to establish his own newspaper. It was at this point that James became involved.

Fraser was acquainted with Harvey J. McFarland, owner of the McFarland Construction Company, who was then the Mayor of Picton. The town had two newspapers – The Picton *Times* and the *Gazette*. The century-old *Times*, a Liberal newspaper was sympathetic to McFarland, but had been experiencing difficulties in generating sufficient advertising revenues to finance the newspaper's operation. The publisher, William McLean, asked McFarland for assistance.

McFarland, with the co-operation of Fraser, agreed to construct a new building in Picton to house a newspaper plant. Fraser would equip it, including the purchase of a new press. It was considered the *Times* would then once again become a profitable enterprise because they would also be printing the *Trentonian* and *Tri-County News.*

Fraser asked James to purchase the printing equipment while McFarland's construction company began to build the new printing plant on King Street. While James was engaged in learning the printing and publishing business he was not, however, able to spend much time at his warehouse business in Trenton, which was, on a day to day basis, being looked after by his brother, Babe.

McLean moved into the new plant in 1956. However, he was unable to cope with his new environment and he moved out again, taking the equipment he had brought to the venture with him back to his former Main Street location. The *Times* continued to be published for a few more years but was to cease publication with its March 16, 1962 edition. The newspaper was then in its 109th year.

After McLean withdrew from the business, James had to replace McLean's equipment and find a manager for the printing plant to ensure the *Trentonian* could continue to publish. James had already opened an office in Trenton with advertising and circulation people, and had hired an editor and reporting staff.

"As I look back, this had to be one of my most difficult business challenges but we published our first issue on Dec. 20, 1956," James said. "It became apparent to me that it was going to be very costly to operate a printing plant in Picton for printing a Trenton newspaper. The decision was made to build a new plant in Trenton. Construction was started in early 1957."

The Trenton plant was to be built at the corner of Quinte and Stewart Streets. James, with the assistance of his brother, Babe, was to supervise both the construction and the equipping of the plant. It was completed and operating within six months and the *Trentonian* immediately went from one to two issues a week. The demands of the newspaper increasingly took James away from his warehouse business and involved him in much time-consuming travel. It was to have a negative impact on the growth of Trenton Cold Storage as James had to look after his warehouse business interests on evenings and weekends.

"But I also hasten to say that what I learned in establishing the publishing business was a great education for dealing with business matters in general."

The first two-section, 12-page issue of the *Trentonian* sold for 5¢ a copy and home delivery was provided. Neither Fraser's nor James' name appeared on the masthead, the publisher being listed as Tri-County Publications Limited. Burton Lewis was editor and general manager and James Muir, news editor.

In July, 1961, James was able to deliver to Fraser the files and circulation list of the *Courier-Advocate*, a purchase completed for $10,000. The *Courier-Advocate* was amalgamated into the *Trentonian*.

"At this time the Senator had been suffering from Parkinson's disease, which had been coming on slowly for almost 10 years. He was very pleased that this battle was over but as I look back I think it was a letdown for him because he had reached the stage where there were no more battles. I felt that he began to lose interest."

The *Daily-Times Gazette* of Oshawa described the new newspaper as a credit to the town and its publisher, "it being produced in an excellent printing plant with a high level of craftsmanship." Former Trenton resident Harry Moore, writing in The *Pembroke Observer*, predicted the newspaper would be one to be "reckoned with in the life of the airforce town in the days to come."

Moore said he knew the Trenton newspaper story as few knew it. "We have known all the publishers, P.J. O'Rourke, Clarence Young, Vance Statia, Thomas Jarrett and those who were to follow them. At 22 we were foremen of The *Courier* for Clarence Young. That was in 1904. We held the same job for the same man for a time in late 1916, but 17 years later, after the two town papers had been amalgamated, we returned to become owner. That was July 1, 1933."

"Originally, Trenton had two weeklies. The Conservative *Advocate,* established in 1854; the Liberal *Courier,* established in 1862 and printed on one of the first cylinder presses imported into Ontario. The two papers were amalgamated in the 20's, at which time a third paper, The *Quinte Sun*, made its first appearance."

Moore said he had heard the new newspaper had "sound financial backing" and he predicted that it would be "eminently successful."

McFarland, also owned property in Trenton and was, at the time, involved in a lawsuit with the Town of Trenton over the deeding of streets on his property adjacent to the Central Bridge Co., Ltd. Trenton Cold Storage was also engaged in an action against the town of Trenton, claiming $15,000 in damage had been caused to its plant through a sewage overflow. Raw sewage had been dumped into the slipway, a private waterlot, with the result that cooling condensers were damaged.

Fraser's involvement in the newspaper was generally known and Mayor Ross Burtt, speaking at the South Hastings Conservative Convention held in Belleville in February, 1957 suggested the editor spoke factionally and implied Senator Fraser influenced the content.

"Indeed, unless the senator possesses a much better crystal ball than I have ever seen in action," wrote editor Lewis, "he has no more advance knowledge than you do, Mayor Burtt Ross, of anything that is to be said in the *Trentonian,* nor has he influenced a word that has appeared in the paper so far."

Nevertheless, the *Trentonian* provided Fraser with considerable agreeable press coverage including favourably reporting his efforts to develop new parks in town and to change the face of Quinte Street by persuading the government to build a new federal building that would also house the post office. The post office was never to be built in this locality, however, because of a change in government.

The Bata Company named a street in Batawa, Fraser Drive, in recognition of the help Fraser had provided to the company when they first settled their plant in Canada. The newspaper provided generous coverage of the event. Anthony Cehota, Bata's director of technical research, said Fraser was, "one man to whom we look upon as the personification of Canadian friendship – rough and tough on the surface, but with a golden heart and understanding under it."

The rumour mill still connected Senator Fraser with the *Trentonian* and the editor, in his column, Speaking for Myself, commented on the "Plague of bickering".

"No town needs to waste its time arguing with or worrying about the snipers, snarlers, pettifoggers and cheap poltroons in its midst. All it needs to do is turn away from them and let them wither on the vine. Or to express it otherwise, the way to end gutter brawls is to get up out of the gutter."

"In general the intent of the rumours has been to portray The *Trentonian* as the 'tool' of some faction or partisan interest – as a 'kept newspaper' dedicated to some similar purpose."

In April, 1957 The Brighton *Ensign* was purchased by Tri-County Publications Ltd., and amalgamated with The *Trentonian*. The Ensign had been founded in 1871. Just 15 years later it was acquired by Charles Albert Lapp. In succession his son Clarence Taylor Lapp, edited and published the newspaper and it was carried on by his daughter, Miss Margaret Rose Lapp.

In June, 1957, The *Trentonian* moved its production department from Picton to the new building in Trenton. For the first time the newspaper was produced entirely in Trenton. In Picton, James had learned the newspaper and printing business from the ground up even losing the tips of two fingers in a printing press, one week before he was to be married. Between 1957 and 1960 the newspaper progressed from flatbed printing to letterpress rotary and then to off-set rotary printing. The award-winning newspaper introduced full colour pictures and went to three issues a week.

In 1957, Eben James married Gwendolyn Mayne. The Senator, who had often required Eben to drive him around immediately called upon Eben's wife to carry out this task so that James had more time to devote to the newspaper as well as to his cold storage company.

After the battle between Fraser and Sisson was over and the *Trentonian* well established he appeared to lose interest in his affairs. The pugnacious character so familiar to James was no more. The Senator died in October, 1963 and a new chapter opened in James' life when he became involved as an executor for Fraser's complex estate, and took over management of the Fraser farm as well as operating Trenton Cold Storage.

Eben and Babe, who had lost their father at a very young age, had now lost their mentor. Fraser had been difficult to work with at times but the

James brothers had learned much from the old man, who had had a very keen understanding of human nature.

"The pugnacious old man that I had come to know and respect was no more. I found myself as an executor, along with the Senator's long time private secretary Jim Cox and the Guarantee Trust Company, looking after the Senator's estate. His estate consisted of stocks and bonds in the seven figures, a one thousand-acre farm operation and the Cooperage property in downtown Trenton. His wife who was being maintained at home with 24 hour nursing care was not well and this was another facet of an executor's responsibility."

At James' suggestion, Cox moved into the Cold Storage office. "We closed out the Senator's office, which made it easier for me to spend more time with our warehousing business. Cox gathered up the securities, catalogued them along with the properties and sent them to the corporate executor, the Guarantee Trust Company. I was responsible for looking after the farm, which consisted of more than 200 acres of orchard, 160 head of beef cattle along with all the ramifications that come with that kind of farming operation."

It was necessary for James to become familiar with the management of the farm, finish the harvesting of the apple crop and to find markets for this produce. Cliff Cochrane was the farm manager. He was an elderly man who was ready for retirement and he had stayed with the Senator because he had been with him for more then 30 years. Now that the Senator was gone, Cochrane's enthusiasm for the farm was waning.

Under the terms of the will, an investment company was established which included the farm and all the real estate holdings along with the liquid assets that were part of the farm operation. James was to be appointed General Manager at a salary of $25,000 per year plus car and expenses. The Trust Company was in control for 15 years and the farm was to be operated for that period of time. At the end of the period, the assets would be divided 50% for Eben, 25% for Babe, and 25% for Nick Fraser.

"Cox was very supportive but he felt my situation was intolerable. He said he had spent a lifetime working with the Senator trying to move any funds he could to the farm operation to keep it out of the red. His advice was to get rid of the farm but that was not possible. Cox predicted the farm would eat up the estate and probably use up me in the process.

"Looking back, I threw myself into the farming business, became involved with the Asparagus Growers Marketing Board, was a founding member of the Ontario Apple Marketing Commission and started to experience first hand the farming communities' mentality."

James was also a director of the Ontario Food Processors Association and was President of this association in 1989.

"The Senator once told me that farming was the most difficult business he had been in and to make a farm profitable was a challenge. After a very short time, I realized that what he said was an understatement. I did not know why he had wanted to do this to me."

James accepted the situation and tried to make the best of it. He found the farm had insufficient apple storage and these facilities had to be built. This produced some revenue but the apple storage business was not one in which James wanted to become involved.

"It became apparent in the early 1970's that the farm would not produce enough revenue to cover its shortfall and we constructed low temperature warehousing at the farm to offset this revenue shortfall."

James considered expanding his newspaper interests and pondered the practicality of area daily newspapers amalgamating with one company publishing all the daily newspapers between Napanee and Port Hope. He could not interest other publishers in this idea, however, and in 1963 the *Trentonian* was sold to Thompson Newspapers.

"The *Trentonian* was one of the few papers that was printed on a web off-set system using cold type, at the time, and the Thompson Company was very interested in acquiring it.

"After the *Trentonian* was sold, Babe and I put all our efforts into our warehousing business finding customers who required our services. The best way to do this, we found, was to persuade food processing industries to locate in Trenton and we were successful in doing that. My reason for bringing industry to Trenton was not the same as the Senator's. Fraser was interested in creating jobs and building the town's industrial core. I was bringing in industries that would be allied with the warehousing business."

When Eben James II first worked at the cold storage plant, product was moved on a pushcart. "It required a strong back and a lot of paperwork to get it from the warehouse to the customer. Today, our customer keys in the order on a computer in their sales office, it is read on a terminal mounted on a fork truck on the warehouse floor, and the fork truck operator collects the product from the storage area and places it in bays to be loaded."

CHAPTER 21

Proud of the past –
Looking towards the future

Founder Eben James I would certainly recognize the company's head office were it possible for him to return. But he would undoubtedly be astounded to see the extent of the company's growth and its development into a full-service, fully integrated logistics provider delivering large volumes of foodstuffs from their manufacturing and warehousing areas to markets across the country – a reliable supply chain stretching across Canada.

"We take food from where it is made and get it to where it is consumed, whether in Canada or the United States," states Eben James III, President and Chief Executive Officer of the TCS Group of Companies. "As far as where it is made, we have foodstuffs that originate from all over the world. And we can arrange for pick up anywhere in the world."

Many foodstuff manufacturers have established plants in Trenton (Quinte West) at or near TCS warehouses in order to effect savings by not having to ship their products long distances from the point of manufacture to storage and distribution facilities.

"The operation of the company's juice plant, for instance, is entirely paid for by the savings of not having to ship water from the United States, as would be the case if the finished product was shipped here for distribution. We receive concentrate from Florida and South America and change the state of the produce here for the Canadian market. This is an example where we are involved in a small manufacturing operation to take costs out of the supply chain."

The TCS Group looks after the transportation and the storage of products produced by many companies and corporations, both large and small. In some company alliances, TCS has become involved in financing a customer's inventory.

"We also have the technology in place to recall products from the market place should it be necessary. We have the information system to know where every box has been delivered."

The TCS Group operation is similar to the hub and spoke system used by many airlines.

For many years, the company mainly distributed goods manufactured in Eastern Canada across Canada and particularly in Ontario, Quebec and the

Three generations

Maritimes. In recent years, products manufactured elsewhere in Canada have been stored and distributed by the TCS Group. A warehouse was opened in Edmonton, (TCS Alberta Inc.) to assemble frozen and chilled foods for regional distribution in the west. It also allows foodstuffs manufactured in the west to be economically distributed to the east. This has opened up a field and market that the company has, historically, not served.

The company is considering establishment of another distribution hub in British Columbia, strengthening its presence in the west. A storage and distribution center may also be built in the Maritimes. In time, the company expects to reach down into the United States.

"Strategically, we have the ability to deliver in every single part of Canada and we have the infrastructure to do that." Mr. James said. "The other strategy we are attempting to employ is to continue to reduce the economic dependence we have on any one company. One way we are doing that is by expanding the business. We continue to hunt aggressively for new business and to make strategic alliances with food manufacturers to locate their manufacturing facilities on site. This reduces the logistical costs of shipping from the manufacturing plant to the storage point. If we do this with all sorts of foodstuffs, the gamut is huge."

TCS is a privately owned company managed by the third generation of the same family. The three generations of James' have always been very concerned with the well being of the people employed by their companies.

"It is important to us that the people we work with are caring

John Blair

people," Mr. James said. "We usually hire people who know absolutely nothing about this business and then teach and train them. It is more important to us to hire people who care about the customer, their fellow workers, their homes, families and the community in which they live than that they, initially, are familiar with this type of business. It's really important to us and that is why we have incorporated the words 'we care' in our company logo."

Eben W. O. James has a different management style than his father and grandfather. Both founder Eben James and the second Eben James – who is chairman of the board – ran their enterprises directly. Eben III manages the company in co-operation with an executive or "leadership" committee and all major decisions are made by consensus, even though decisions are more difficult to make when a consensus is required.

The committee consists of Chief Executive Officer Eben James III, secretary-treasurer S. A. (Stan) Bigford and vice-president, Operations, John Blair. All must agree before any major decisions are made. A fourth member of the executive committee was Craig Kitchener, vice president, Sales and Marketing, until his lamented and premature death in December, 2004. A past member of the management committee, now retired, was Al Borthwick, for many years senior vice-president of the company.

Eben James III grew up in the business. As a child, he often accompanied his father to the plant on weekends and the company was often a topic at the dinner table. From about the age of 15, Eben III spent his summer holidays at the main plant and subsidiary plants. His first job was helping to load and unload the rail cars that, at that time, ran on a spur line adjacent to the main warehouse. He also swept floors and moved pallets around the plant.

"I remember being very conscious that I had to not only keep up but to work as hard as I could as many people felt my job was a privilege of association and not one obtained by merit. I was very conscious that I had to set the pace."

Another summer Eben James III worked with Ralph Adams in the Maintenance Department, where he did painting and cleaning, oiled

Stan Bigford

compressors and worked on evaporators. In the last summer before leaving for University he worked at Produce Processors under Don Firth.

"I qualified as an engineer and got my engineer's papers that summer. Rick Selman, Rick Sharpe and Dave Wannamaker indoctrinated me by having me clean out the Napanee boiler. I can remember being totally black from head to toe – you could just see the whites of my eyes.

Eben III started in economics, financial and administrative studies at the University of Western Ontario in 1981 to obtain the pre-requisites necessary to get into a School of Business. He was accepted at Brock University. He also applied to the University of Western Ontario School of Business and the Schulich School of Business at York University. He was accepted at Brock University but let the offer of acceptance expire in hope of getting into the University of Western Ontario.

In early August, he learned he was not accepted into the University of Western Ontario School of Business. The only option left was York's Schulich School of Business.

"My father had told me to 'sell myself' to the admissions officer at the Schulich School of Business. I was referred to Charmaine Curtis (I later learned she had the nickname of 'The Barracuda') and she asked me why she should let me into her business school. I said I wanted the education and that I wanted to learn, as that would assist me with our small family business. She hummed and hawed and said she would have to think about it and emphasized even if she said yes, it would only be 'a conditional acceptance'."

"I left the office knowing I had given it the best shot I could. On August 19 I received an offer of admission to the Honours Bachelor of Business Administration program at York University. They only accept 120 people a year. I remember my ego got pumped up big time – I had been told that some 2,000 people a year try to get acceptance into the program"

Eben James III graduated in 1985 with an honours degree. He decided he wanted to do two things: attend a graduate school for his Master's degree (MBA) and also obtain some practical business experience. He went on to

Al Borthwick

graduate school at Schulich and graduated in 1986 with a Master's Degree in Business Administration.

Upon graduation, he interviewed with three large Canadian companies but, at the last moment, decided to continue working at Trenton Cold Storage where his father was seeking a Controller.

At this time, Eben was also offered a position with an American company but if he accepted this employment he would have to commit to a minimum of five years with them. "After careful consideration of the offer I decided to continue working in my father's company."

"During the time I was at university my father had received two offers to sell the company. He turned the offers down but as I was considering staying at TCS I needed to decide on my future. I loved the Trenton area and preferred to stay there. And, in the back of my mind, I always wanted to perpetuate this business – I knew what I would be doing, although I had felt I might have benefited first from some outside experience."

John Blair, Vice-President, Operations, declares that a company cannot stand still. "You must either grow or you shrink." The company's expansion into the west through the purchase of the former Gainers meat and packing plant at 66th Street and Yellowhead Trail was not without problems, he said.

"Edmonton is the fastest growing city in Canada and has the highest number of food processing companies in the province. Because of the tremendous growth in Edmonton in both the oil and high-technology areas it was found that construction costs were high and contractors were scarce. It was also difficult to find, and keep, skilled workers."

The new warehouse facility was operating well within two years of opening and the staff has now grown to over 50 people.

"In Edmonton, as at the various company locations in Trenton the emphasis has been on maintaining the family atmosphere, a policy successfully maintained by Eben James II, his late brother Mawnan (Babe) and continued by the present Chief Executive Officer. Blair, who has a degree in mechanical engineering, recalled that when Babe James first met with him he expected the interview would last for an hour or two.

"The interview lasted all day. Not only did he interview me but he also spent a lot of time getting to know me. He took me around to all the plants and introduced me to many people. I saw that the people were pleased to see him and I could see that the James family was concerned about their people. This swayed my decision to join the company. I was, at that time, working with Canadian General Electric in Montreal."

Initially hired in 1984 as plant engineer for Produce Processors he soon became responsible for engineering and maintenance work throughout Trenton Cold Storage and associated companies. In 1995 he was appointed Vice President, Operations, responsible for all facilities and the company's Human Resources Department.

Stan Bigford, Secretary-treasurer and Chief Financial Officer, says the company's evolution has largely revolved around technology. "TCS is well known as a very responsive organization. We make changes very rapidly and also such things as the construction of new facilities. We have a lot of potential for growth." He sees more strategic alliances being made with food manufacturers and longer-term alliances with customers.

"The reason for longer term commitments is the tremendous investments in technology that are necessary – huge investments of capital. We are intensively focused on providing the service. We take no profit on the product."

The success of Trenton Cold Storage and its affiliated companies is due to the management's ability to change to meet the times, similar to the way that founder Eben James I adapted his business to cope with two World Wars and setbacks that had been caused by the worldwide Depression in the 1930s. The three generations of the James family have always believed in any capital spending that could improve efficiency. Management has also adapted well to new ideas and plant and equipment have always been kept at the cutting edge of new technology. In recent years, high-speed communication technology has reshaped TCS operations.

Over the years, the three Ebens – grandfather, father and son, have been responsible for much of the industrial development in Trenton (now Quinte West) by persuading foodstuff companies to locate in the town. Senator William Fraser, Eben I's wife's brother was also responsible for much of Trenton's growth, by encouraging and assisting various companies, to locate in the town and area.

Companies are like people – they all have a certain life span but this can be extended by adjusting and adapting to changing times. While some 30 per cent of all family owned businesses in Canada survive into the second generation only 12 per cent make it into the third.

The TCS Group of companies has survived and prospered over the past century because the three generations of the James family have all sought excellence as avidly as they have sought profit. The company's family legacy has been a valuable asset because the best leaders are empire builders who want to create something that will outlast them. The present CEO has the ability to analyze a problem quickly and critically and then move on to implement the solution.

TCS has been and remains a socially responsible company very involved in the betterment and growth of the community. In fact, for the past 100 years the history of Eben James I and his descendants has been entwined with much of the history of this historic community. The James family has overwhelmingly been a positive force in the development of Trenton.

The TCS Group looks forward to the future and its second century with confidence in its services, its people and its management.

EPILOGUE

The TCS Group

There is nostalgia for the past for many people and it is hoped that this book will recall a little of what had been lost to time. The loss of the old does not always equate to progress. If we wish to understand our present we must hold a light to the past.

Although much information about the company's early days has been lost in the mists of time, it is hoped that this volume has captured enough of the past to show how founder Eben James I, a determined and influential man, built up this remarkable, socially responsible and respected Canadian company. The best leaders are empire builders who are determined to create something that will outlive them.

When the company was founded, Canada was still powered by horses and steam. Travel was mainly by horseback, carriage, rail or steamship. This was truly a different world - for someone born in 1901, life expectancy was 56. Canada was only 34 years old with seven provinces. Alberta and Saskatchewan would be born in 1905.

It was a dangerous world. Milk was not pasteurized. Diseases, such as tuberculosis and diphtheria, were killers. Antibiotics were far in the future. Trenton had gravel roads, board sidewalks and when it rained, mud everywhere.

Just 100 years ago in real time, but an age in comparison to the cultural and technological realities of today.

During some of the difficult times in the past – the Depression Years and two World Wars – the company survived only because of the persistent flame of hope that burned in the mind of company founder, Eben James I.

Trenton Cold Storage looks back at over a century of caring business with justifiable pride.

In this century, the TCS Group faces new challenges and must continue to change and adapt – as did the first Eben James – to the demands of the future. As Thomas Bata comments in his book, Bata Shoemaker to the World, "None of us has a crystal ball to tell us what the future may bring, and entrepreneurs who aren't willing to ride out occasional storms had better not venture beyond their home turf."

But one thing will not change at TCS – the philosophy of caring. The management recognizes the debt it owes to all those people who, over the years, through their skills and talents, have helped to build this company.

The TCS Centennial banquet was held on Friday, November 8, 2002.

Above from left: Eben James III; Archie McLean, guest speaker; Mawnen (Babe) James; Quinte West Mayor Robert R.J. Campney; Eben James II.

Left: M.C. Roy Bonisteel

Bottom left: Eben James III presents Mayor Campney with a municipal Chain of Office.

Hon. Col. Eben James II, 2 Air Movements Squadron, 8 Wing, CFB Trenton.

Below: A memorial stone at St. George's Cemetery, Trenton, dedicated to those who died while training under the British Commonwealth Air Training Plan at RCAF Trenton during the Second World War. The monument and extensive landscaping around the Commonwealth veteran's plots was undertaken as a TCS Centennial project.

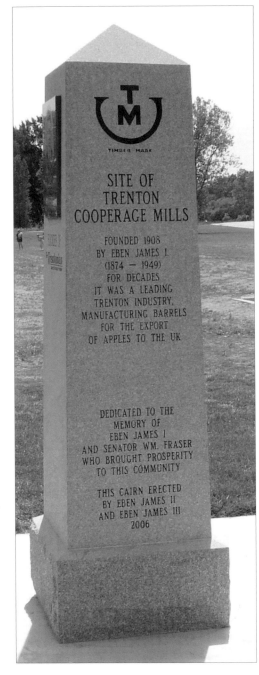

A cairn was erected on the former site of Trenton Cooperage Mills in September, 2006 and dedicated to Eben James I and Senator Wm. Fraser.

As the family-owned company reached its 100th year, CEO and President Eben James III changed the company logo to include the words "We Care". He said: "It means we care about our customers, not only in the services we provide for them, but in how we execute the delivery of these services. It means we care about each other. It means we care about our community, our homes and our families…we care means doing the best we can every day in all we do."

Overwhelmingly, founder James was a positive force in the development of Trenton. And his sons, Eben II, Mawnan (Babe), and grandson, Eben III, continued in the same way, contributing wholeheartedly to the community, becoming involved in its growth and development, and donating to its progress in countless ways.

During the company's centennial year many commemorative events were held for both customers and staff, including a boat cruise on the Bay of Quinte. At a memorable Centennial banquet with Roy Bonisteel as master of ceremonies, a new chain of office was presented to Quinte West Mayor R.J. (Bob) Campney

Additionally, as a lasting reminder of the celebrations, the company funded a major restoration of St. George's Cemetery in Trenton where many Second World War airmen are buried. An impressive granite memorial was erected and dedicated to the memory of those who died during the Second World War while training under the British Commonwealth Air Training Plan at the Royal Canadian Air Force base at Trenton. Eben James II and Lt. Gen. A Chester Hull (Ret'd) unveiled the monument. The cairn was dedicated by the Rector Rev. James McShane, assisted by Padre Sid Horne. St. George's Cemetery Board sponsored the ceremony in conjunction with 413 (Air Force City) Wing, Air Force Association of Canada, and the Royal Canadian Legion, Branch 110, Trenton. No. 8 Wing, Concert Band, pipes and drums, took part in the ceremony by permission of Col. David Higgins, wing commander of 8 Wing, CFB Trenton.

Finally, as a commitment to the community it has called home for 100 years, the TCS Group carried out extensive renovations on Fraser Park and assisted in the relocation of the War Memorial to a new site between the park and the Royal Canadian Legion.

TCS has also contributed to restoration work at St. George's Anglican Church – the town's oldest and most historic building. The first Eben James had been a warden of this church and chose the memorial stained glass window to honour those who fell in the First World War.

On Sept. 9, 2005, Eben James II was commissioned as the Honorary Colonel of 2 Air Movements Squadron at 8 Wing, Canadian Forces Base, Trenton. This was in acknowledgment of his logistical expertise and also recognition of his support for the military.

Today, the TCS Group is a highly efficient, diversified and results-oriented company. It caters its logistics business to the food makers and purveyors of the world. Its success a result of its highly motivated team.

This book is intended to honour the founder, his successors and all people connected with this progressive company and to challenge the new generation to even greater achievements.

*"Who that sets forth upon a voyage of discovery
ever knows whither he may be carried?"*

- Dr. Jessopp of Norwich, England
Clergyman, schoolmaster and historian.

Mawnen "Babe" James
One of God's gentlemen

Babe James

Named for the Cornish village where his parents once lived for a time, Mawnen Fraser James would be known throughout his life as "Babe".

Born on August 29, 1930, in the family home at 108 Henry Street, Trenton, he was the youngest child of Eben James I and his wife, Jeanie Fraser. As the youngest of the couple's four children, he was always referred to as "the baby", an appellation eventually shortened simply to "Babe".

A flaxen-haired boy of delicate constitution, he had pneumonia three times, before reaching the age of three. At eight, he developed rheumatic fever. His mother nursed him diligently, because of his frailty and became highly protective of him. She refused to cut his hair, until school authorities told him the other boys were sending him to the girls' entrance.

Babe grew up in Trenton, where he attended Dufferin Street School. As a young man, he enrolled in Trinity College in Port Hope. His father had married late in life. By the time Babe reached his fifth birthday his father was more than 60 years of age. Still, he taught his son to sail and to make sails. An accomplished equestrian, he also gave him riding lessons. He was determined to teach Babe these skills, just as a much younger father would have done.

In 1949, Eben James I died. Two years later, Babe left school to join the family firm. Initially, he worked in the shipping office. Later, he transferred to the compressor plant, taking it from a manual operation to a sophisticated, automated system. He had a natural gift for machinery and electronics.

He was self-taught, liked people and understood how they wanted to be treated. Babe had the ability to put people at ease and knew each of the family firm's workers by name. If one of them had problems, he took time to learn about their circumstances and did what he could to help.

Babe was vice-president of the family firm, when in the early 1990's, he began to experience difficulties in remembering. He was subsequently diagnosed as having the onset of Alzheimer's disease. Babe realized his problem and tried to compensate for lapses of memory, when he was with his friends and colleagues. He continued to participate in all of the family and community activities that had always meant so much to him.

In time, it became apparent that he was having increasing difficulties in coping with his condition. He told his family that he wanted to live a full life for as long as possible. He continued to visit the office, almost every day. His good humour was infectious and he always had a ready quip for every occasion.

Some people did not realize that Babe had developed Alzheimer's Disease, because he was able to conceal it with his good humour and a desire to put people at ease. In time, he was no longer able to drive, but continued his visits to the office, even when he could no longer remember the workers' names. His wife, Dorothy, would drop him off, every morning to visit and have coffee with his cronies. His friends looked after him and took him home.

The Trenton Cold Storage Group celebrated its 100th anniversary in 2002 and Babe James was present for a centenary banquet held, November 7, to mark the occasion. Later he attended the annual staff Christmas party and derived great pleasure from listening to the music.

A few days before Christmas, Babe attended a Christmas carol concert, featuring the Trenton Citizen's Band. He joined the audience in singing carols and took special pleasure in this outing. Later that evening, he suffered a heart attack. He was hospitalized in Trenton and appeared to be making a recovery.

A week later, while in hospital, he was watching an Anne Murray Christmas special and could not resist singing along. Babe's joy in the music was infectious. Soon, his roommates were enjoying the songs, too.

Babe did not awaken the next day. He died peacefully in his sleep, on December 23, 2002, having spent his last evening doing the thing he enjoyed most – having fun with people.

Services were held on December 30, at St. George's Anglican Church, followed by interment in St. George's Cemetery. Babe James is survived by his wife, the former Dorothy Simmons, daughters Heather (Mrs. Richard Livesley) of Toronto, Melanie James of Toronto and son, Kevin James of Ottawa.

Craig Kitchener
A true sportsman

Craig Kitchener

Craig Kitchener, vice-president Sales and Marketing for the TCS Group, collapsed and died on Saturday, December 4, 2004, while playing in a men's recreation league hockey game in Trenton. He was 41.

Craig had always loved hockey. He joined the Belleville Bulls Hockey Club when the team joined the Ontario Hockey League (OHL). The Belleville Bulls established themselves as one of the most respected franchises in the Ontario Hockey League.

He had been acquired by the Bulls at the beginning of the 1981-82 season from the Oshawa Generals. He scored 19 goals and 33 assists for 52 points in 63 games and added 188 penalty minutes.

His second and final season with the Bulls was even better, with 27 goals, 74 points and 140 penalty minutes.

Former Bulls general manager and head coach Larry Mavety, now general manager of the Kingston Frontenacs said Mr. Kitchener was an excellent junior hockey player.

"He had the size, he could skate and shoot and he was tough. He did everything you could ask...He was a valuable member of our hockey club."

A Toronto native, he was a graduate of Acadia University. He was employed from 1988 to 1991 as a sales representative with Crawford Metals. He joined the Trenton Cold Storage group in 1991 and became vice-president of sales and marketing.

He is survived by his wife, the former Michelle Tilley, daughters Brianna and Charlotte and a son, Joseph.

Services were held on Wednesday, December 8, at Bridge Street United Church, Belleville. Interment took place at Carrying Place Cemetery.

APPENDIX 1

What Life Means to Me

Among the papers of Eben James I was found the following essay. The paper is undated but was written late in his life. Minor editorial changes have been made.

We are told that the star under which we have been born gives to our lives its character. Therefore, I conclude that mine must have been one of hope, because, despite all the obstacles and disappointments I have met with, I am still a practical optimist. I am not living in a dreamy future, but believe that the forces of good and evil are at least equally divided and that life is full of possibilities that I may live to see realized.

My earliest memory takes me back to happy surroundings with the kindest of relations and the best and highest examples one could wish, I never knew a mother's love, losing her when too young to remember. I went early into boarding school, a life common to most English boys above the poorer class. This teaches them early to fight their own battles, think for themselves and be self-reliant. And perhaps also making them reserved in after life yet causing them to meet with the world wide success that has characterized the nation.

Home influence soon existed only in weekly letters (*after he had left for Canada*).

And I learned to struggle against sorrow and enjoy being alone and commence on the "solitary way" which we all go, only perhaps, I did this, earlier in life.

As I grew older, at school, I looked forward, as all youth does, with expectancy and chafed for the time when I should leave and enter the real world, wondering what it had in store for me. I left without many regrets outside of parting from a few particular chums. I have learned since to count my real friends very easily, not that there are not numbers of people I could like, but that we meet only a few in our rapid journey we come to know well.

Up to that period, religion had been taken as a matter of course, as I had been trained, and I never questioned nor doubted or gave it much thought.

Following an occupation in life was a most perplexing question. Never being able to decide on one I, like many others, simply drifted, but endeavored to fill any position that presented itself with the utmost ability that I possessed. Perhaps that fact and a good home influence guided me past many pitfalls.

Often they are the undoing of many people, similarly placed, who got their freedom as early as I did.

As I developed, I studied the men and women I met to learn, if possible, their true character and views and to find out what life really was to others; what was real and what pretended and to arrive at some conclusions both religious and secular. I had read the Scriptures several times and studied the views of the writers pro and con that came under my notice and passed through long periods of religious infidelity

In a few words, life to me is a sphere on which I find myself, like all mankind, wondering whence I came and whither I am going, knowing that my makeup in character and physique is the result of hereditary influences. It is a place where to develop the greatest happiness, I cannot be a drone but must work hard enough to feel that at the end of each day I have left undone nothing I might reasonably have done.

Eben James I in later years.

I must live honestly toward my fellows, not to gain their good opinion, but that by so doing I shall be at peace with myself and not inwardly ashamed. I must never be proud, if in anything, I excel my fellows, nor be envious of their achievements. Being a creature of chance I may have been born more fortunate than they were and I deserve no credit for this. And, not being envious because I believe in the law of compensation and what I might envy might not be good for me. What I envy is, no doubt, made up to me in other ways.

While I believe in the good in all men, I must not be disappointed if sometime this goodness is not apparent or seems to be over-balanced with evil, for the old reason that unfortunate environments of training and breeding have produced that result.

I must endeavour in studying my fellow man to make due allowance for the prejudices that may have surrounded him and beware lest prejudice in myself presents me from seeing the truth. I must strive ever for the truth in all things taking as patterns the best examples, avoiding what appear to be their errors. I must not for any reason sacrifice a principle I believe to be right.

To me, the world is largely a place of wonder and beauty where nature's panoramas are at times enchanting; where the music of the songbirds, the human voice or the music of a great organ can give me happiness indescribable. Where the work of a clever painter, sculptor, or mechanic fills me with admiration and the love of a true friend warms my innermost self.

I can live only in the present but believe that I am greater than the beasts who have their limit, so is the infinite Creator of the universe myriads of times greater than my finite conception. He has created all, whether by evolution or otherwise, so He will bring me to the new stage, or why had He

*Eben James I
with daughter Joan,
in Montreal.*

planted in the human heart of most of us, whether savage or civilized, that belief that we never die?

Apart from the teachings of Scripture whose foreknowledge of events alone would make me believe its inspiration, as well as the effect we see of it in the lives of those who follow it closely. *"What I know not now will be revealed hereafter."*

Further, I believe that all things happen in their appointed time, the discovery of coal, steam, or electricity and the discovery of America for the expansion of the Old World.

I believe that we are free agents and have the option of good or evil, that the former brings happiness to individuals and nations and the latter, disaster.

I believe that I must expect sorrow, it is the order of this present state if only for the reason that we must all age and

That, amid the Babel of religions, one must seek for the truth, do all the good one can and so live, that as Tennyson says, we may have no regrets when we come "to cross the Bar".

APPENDIX 2

Companies in the Trenton Cold Storage Group

Trenton Cold Storage Inc.

TCS Realty Inc.

Fraser Glenburnie Inc.

Tri-County Apple Growers Ltd.

Old Orchard Farms Ltd.

TCS Alberta Inc.

Jampack Limited

Produce Processors Ltd.

TCS Logistics Inc.

TCS Wellington Inc.

1382921 Ontario Inc.

1382922 Ontario Inc.

1382839 Ontario Inc. (Tulsa Limited Partnership)

APPENDIX 3

Mayors of Trenton

Trenton was proclaimed a town on Dominion Day, 1880. For electoral purposes the Act became effective on January 1, 1881 when Dr. H. W. Day became the first mayor.

1882-82	Dr. H.W. Day
1883	Dr. J.B. Moran
1884-85	James Richardson
1886	G.W. Ostrum
1888-89	M.B. Morrison
1890	P.J. O'Rourke
1891	A.W. Hawley
1892-94	Dr. W.S. Jaques
1895-1900	M.B. Morrison
1901	W.R. Phillips
1902-04	Jesse Funnell
1905-07	Dr. E. Kidd
1911-12	Jesse Funnell
1913-14	Dr. E. Kidd
1915	O.E. Fortune
1916-20	W.H. Ireland
1921	Jesse Funnell
1922-23	Lewis Roenigk
1924-30	William A. Fraser
1931-32	Chester W. Lott
1933	Howard D. Graham
1934-39	Harry R. Cory
1940	O.G. Alyea
1941-46	Harry R. Corey
1947-52	Kenneth J. Crouch
1953	R.E. Whitley
1954-59	Ross Burtt
1960-68	D. Jas. MacDonald
1968-73	Duncan MacDonald
1974-78	W. Robert Patrick
1978-82	Duncan MacDonald
1982-97	Neil Robertson
1998-2000	Jack Arthur

Town of Quinte West

2001-	R.J. (Bob) Campney

ACKNOWLEDGEMENTS

First of all I am grateful to Eben James II, chairman of Trenton Cold Storage, Inc., who worked closely with me in the preparation of this book and to the company's President and Chief Executive Officer, Eben W.O. James III.

My thanks to Margot James and Joan Kendall, daughters of Eben James I, and also to Gwen James.

I am indebted to Dorothy James, (the wife of the late Mawnen 'Babe' James), a keen genealogist, for helping to sort letters, documents and photographs, spanning a 60 year period, that were contained in four large steamer trunks where they had remained since the death of the company founder, Eben James I, in 1949.

My appreciation to the staff at Quinte West Library, Trenton, Ont., Prince Edward County Library, (Picton and Bloomfield branches), the L.E. Shore Memorial Library, Thornbury, Ont., and the Prince Edward and Hastings Regiment museum, Belleville, Ont. The Prince Edward County Archives, Picton staff have also shown many courtesies.

Microfilms of The Trenton *Advocate*, The Trenton *Courier*, The Trenton *Courier-Advocate*, the Trenton *Sun*, The Brighton *Ensign* and The *Trentonian* yielded first-hand accounts of past events.

Thanks to Michael Power, publisher of the *Trentonian* and the Belleville *Intelligencer*, and to staff members at the *Trentonian* and the *County Weekly News*, Picton. And to the TCS Group people including R. Alan (Al) Borthwick, senior vice-president; John Blair, vice-president – operations; Stan Bigford, secretary-treasurer; the late Craig Kitchener, vice-president, sales and marketing; and particularly to Linda Forbes, Executive Administrative Assistant.

Many individuals have provided help and I am indebted to the following: Hon. Lyle Vanclief, the former federal Minister of Agriculture, Wayne Simmons, Jack Chiang, John Inrig, Dave Taylor, Pam Noxon, Margaret Haylock, Susan Capon, Charles Keller, Gord Meder, Marie Lawson, Ian Robertson. The portraits reproduced in the colour pages were painted in oils by Michael Walker of Kingston.

Alan R. Capon is the author of *His Faults Lie Gently*, a biography of Sir Sam Hughes; *Everybody Called Him Harvey*, a biography of Mayor Harvey J. McFarland of Picton; *Historic Lindsay*, *Stories of Prince Edward County*, *This House of Healing*, *The Stone Church*, and *A Goodly Heritage* etc. He is the co-author of *Desperate Venture, 50 Years a Country Veterinarian*, *Picton Remembered*, *Deseronto – Then and Now*, *Spencer's Common*.